VOICES FROM

THE BIG HOUSE

 VOICES
FROM THE
BIG HOUSE

EDITED BY

Frank Earl Andrews

AND

Albert Dickens

HARLO PRESS, DETROIT, MICHIGAN

HARLO PRESS, 16721 HAMILTON AVE., DETROIT, MICHIGAN 48203

TO JOHN F. MARION . . .

> *for a million reasons.*

TO BO JINGLES . . .

> *who died for thirty-nine dollars.*

TO LITTLE SHEFFY . . .

> *who died for nothing.*

TO CHIEF EDMONDS . . .

> *not to be confused with other chiefs.*

INTRODUCTION

SINCE THE ATTICA RIOT, THE THANKSGIVING uprising at Rahway, the recent flurry of incidents at Trenton, and the sudden focus of national attention and concern on prisons, many forms of literary expression have begun to seep out from behind the drab stone walls. *Voices from the Big House* is one of them. The book encompasses material from both of New Jersey's major prisons at Rahway and Trenton and is the result of many years of work, by men who are tired of being caricaturized as sleezy-eyed, slope-shouldered individuals, with blood dripping from their claws.

The purpose of *Voices from the Big House* is, aside from obtaining funds to finance more things of this type, not to expose the conditions of prison environment, but to expose the stagnating talent in the prison environment.

And, if for only an instant you feel a twinge of concern for us, an inkling of identification with us, the beginning of a new comprehension about us, then we have indeed accomplished our purpose. Perhaps *Voices from the Big House* will only be the forerunner of bigger and better things.

—The Editors

CONTENTS

Voices from the Big House

VOICES FROM

THE BIG HOUSE

HONKY TONK BUD
#00001

Honky Tonk Bud was first related to me by Frank (Bo Jingles) Edwards while I was serving thirty days in Annandale Reformatory's "grave." Since Annandale, and during the course of numerous stints in various jails, I have heard the ode recited over and over again. For the last four years, Dick and I have been trying to trace the origin of this legendary personage, but to no avail. However, from the bits and pieces we did manage to gather, indications are that "Bud" was created in the segregation unit at Bordentown Reformatory.

As Noyes and his "Highwayman" are to the British, as Thayer's "Casey at the Bat" is to Americans, so too has "Honky Tonk Bud" taken his inerasible place, but in the folklore of the prison society. This collection wouldn't be complete without him.

—F. E. A.

AN ODE TO HONKY TONK BUD

Author Unknown

Honky Tonk Bud, the hip-cat stud
Stood digging a game of pool.
He was sharp in his silk bag, but he wasn't no brag
Because he knew he was looking real cool.
He was choked up tight in a white-on-white
And his cocoa-brown suit was down.
He wore a candy-striped tie that hung down to his fly
And he was sporting a gold dust crown.

It was the fifteenth frame of a nine-ball game
And Bud stood watching the play.
With an idle shrug he suddenly dug
A strange cat coming his way.
It was a funny-time cat, wearing a funny-time hat
That must have been five years old.
He wore a wrinkled vine and needed a shine
And shivered as if he were cold.

Now to all the other studs, except Honky Tonk **Bud**,
The stranger looked like an ordinary flunky.
But with well-trained eyes, from many past **highs,**
Bud dug that he was a junky.
Just like that he knew where it was at;
The stranger wanted to get high.
He was sick and needed a fix,
And was out to make a buy.

Bud grinned, as the cat moved in,
And asked him if he knew Shorty Moore.
Now Shorty wasn't around, 'cause his stash was **down;**
He had gone uptown to score.
"But if you got eyes to cop king-size,
I can cop some stuff for you,
'Cause I'm Honky Tonk Bud, the hip-cat stud,
Known from Times Square to Lenox Avenue.
So if you want to cop let's talk shop;
It's the only connection I know.
Give me the bread and lay here dead,
And wait for me to show."

The stranger looked down with a halfway frown,
Trying to make up his mind.
"I'm leery," he said, "to part with this bread;
I'm looking for the best I can find.
'Cause three other cats got cash in the hat
And I don't want to chance their dough.
So cop me a test bag and if the stuff ain't no drag
Then I'll let the bread go."

Bud hesitated, because he'd under-rated,
And thought to make a quick sting.

But the stranger was down; he wasn't no clown;
So he'd have to cop the real thing.
"Tell you what, my man," Bud said, holding up his hand,
"I'll get you a piece, on a short term lease,
And you don't have to put up no ends.
First you can try it; if you like it you buy it—
Either way we'll still be friends."

Bud showed back quick, cause he was also getting sick
And they went up to his pad to fix.
He unwrapped two spikes, laid out two hypes,
And prepared to relieve his heaves.
Then he cooked up the smack, from a cellophane pack,
And they both rolled up their sleeves.

Because his arm was scarred, the stranger hit hard
As he tried to find a vein.
Then he hit red, and Honky said,
"Be cool fool, that stuff's grain."
With the smack tasted, the stranger was wasted.
"That stuff sure enough is nice."
Then the gleam in his eyes, withered and died.
And turned to cold-glazed ice.

Honky Tonk sighed and slowly untied.
"Man, I'm flying real high."
The stranger made a pass, flashed a gold-colored badge,
Said, "Punk, I'm the F.B.I.
The stuff was nice, but it's linked with vice
And it's against the law, you know.
So shut up your trap; put on your wrap;
Grab your hat and let's go."

All the hustlers heard about Honky Tonk's fall, and
Filled the courtroom and also the hall,
For Honky Tonk Bud was a well-liked name,
Because he never hollered and always followed,
The rules of any man's game.
There was Sweet Drawers Lucy, looking real juicy;
Half Head and Stumbling Blue;
Short Cow Dave and his half-breed slave;
And Frenchy, the wandering Jew;
Jo Jo the Rabbit, the hustling girl's habit;
Dumb-Dumb and Cabbage Head;
Sixty-Nine Lil, with Three Dollar Bill;
Cat Eyes and Whiskey-Top Ed.
All eyes turned right, when old Soft Toned Ike
Walked in wearing a new cashmere vine;
While a famous gunslinger, called Sammy the Stinger
Covered him well from behind.

Bud stood cool and unshaken, as the court-oath was taken,
And while the charges were read by the clerk.
Then old Judge Stern, who was known to be firm,
Started the trial with a smirk.
"Now let us proceed; how do you plead
To these indictments of selling junk?"
"Not guilty," said Bud, the hip-cat stud.
"The charges were chumped from the jump."

The D.A., Paul Grace, presented the government's case,
And the agent involved took the stand.
He told in detail how he'd gotten the sale
And that Bud was a big time man.

He's got an adding machine mind; wears a hundred dollar
    vine;
Drives a Caddy as long as a train.
He might act like a squirrel, but he's pimping five girls,
And is a master of the confidence game.

Percival Spence, the hip-cat's defense
Was known as an all time great.
In his hand lay Bud's ten grand,
And also the threads of his fate.
"I can't beat it," he said, as he counted the bread;
"That's a fact you might as well face.
Edgar J. Pagent, the narco agent,
Has built up an airtight case.
Your record's too long; their game is too strong;
And I can't buy a break nowhere.
The jury picking is done; I can't get to a one;
The lab technicians won't buy.
The D.A. is scared and won't take no bread,
And you just don't buy the F.B.I.
I've tried other things, pulled political strings,
But the word is 'hands off'; no can do.
I'm sorry Bud, but that's the rub;
They're out to make an example of you."

These were the facts, as the D.A. attacked
The character of Honky Tonk Bud.
The hustlers sneered, as they heard his name smeared,
Trampled and dragged through the mud.
But all the while, through the storm of the trial,
Honky sat unperturbed.

Voices from the Big House

They squared his name and ranked his game,
And he didn't even say a word

The jury went out, for a twelve-hour bout,
And the foreman, a dirt-farmer named Hodge,
So gravely concerned, announced on return
The defendant was guilty as charged.

The hustlers screamed frame, called the jury some names;
A few even voiced a threat.
Then old Judge Stern, who was known to be firm,
Banged for order with his mallet.
The hustlers quelled and a sudden hush fell,
So silent in wonder that it sounded like thunder.
The judge cleared his throat and asked Bud by rote,
"Does the defendant have something to say?"
"I do," said Bud, the hip-cat stud, "before you send me
        away."

"Now I'm not crying, cause the agent's lying
And left you all with the notion
That I'm a big wheel in the narcotics field.
I hope he cops a promotion.
I knew from the jump, you was holding the trump
When you wouldn't let my lawyer object.
A fact is a fact and a stack is a stack,
And I couldn't make you shuffle the deck.
I'll get a full load, 'cause I strayed from the code.

You'll make an example of me
While some drunken villain, runs over your children,
Pays a small fine and goes free.

20

But just the same, it's all in the game;
I knew when I sat down to play,
I took all the odds; you dealt all the low cards;
But that's the price a junky must pay.
So here's a note, for your reporters to quote—
Bud took his time with a grin—
But those that know, they'll tell you for sure
It's the same kind of grin when I win."

HERMAN LOUIS McMILLAN
#36957

About a year ago, after exhausting his last legal appeal, Mac took a vow of silence and hasn't opened his mouth since. Before that time he was a poet and a writer, and four of his poems were published in a collection titled Negro Voices, *by Julian Messner. He also had a story published in* Black World *titled, "The Day Little Moses Spoke." Mac is currently in the New Jersey State Hospital, undergoing whatever it is they undergo down there. We hope he finds his way back soon.*

WHAT GOES AROUND COMES AROUND

by

Herman Louis McMillan

NEEDLE-LIKE RAINDROPS SHOT DOWN SHARPLY from a slate colored sky and stung Hapless Jones' charcoal cheeks. When a blast of February wind whipped up under his raggedy army surplus jacket, he cursed under his breath and turned into Big Mama's Cafe Table D'hote De Pig.

He closed the door and leaned against it, sighing in ecstasy when the warmth started thawing the icicles on the end of his tangled goatee. He looked around the interior of Big Mama's, a dank, gloomy greasy spoon, with a row of paint-chipped booths running opposite a battered wooden counter. The first thing he took note of was a wild looking individual in the last booth, near a door that led into Big Mama's kitchen. It was a brother, squatting on top of the table in his birthday suit, shaking his head from side to side and mumbling incoherent nothings.

What really captured Hapless' attention was the dude reclining in the first booth. He was as out of place in Big Mama's as a rose bud in a manure pile. He sported a shimmering cocoa brown bag, that matched his smooth complexion, and a shirt that was a mass of elegant green ruffles. A blue sapphire winked from his right pinkie; a diamond watch sparkled on his left wrist; and even the dim light failed to hide the spit shine on the tips of his brown flyweights.

"You got eye trouble, baby?"

Hapless shook his head and came off the door, sockless feet squishing inside the weatherbeaten tennis shoes he wore. The clean dressed brother reeked of prosperity and he figured if he could work the Jeff Game right, he might be able to pick up enough for a meal. He grinned, showing two rows of big white teeth, and slid into the booth.

"Naw, man. Just digging de bags. What kinda material is dat anyway?"

"You wouldn't believe me if I told you."

"How come?"

"Nobody ever does."

"Tell me anyway."

The well dressed dude took a cigarette from a platinum case and fitted it into a jade holder. He lit it with a matching platinum lighter and blew out a cloud of opium-like smoke, then he peered at Hapless for a long moment. "The threads was weaved by a herd of brown assam silk worms. The kicks was handmade from the tender sides of ten thousand click beetles, and the shirt was spun from crushed palm fronds."

Hapless made a face in spite of himself. The well dressed dude dug it.

"Suppose you tell me where you got your kicks from?"

Hapless focused his attention on a cockroach that was crawling under Big Mama's food counter. "I'm up pretty tight right now, but I'll be back on my feet soon. I got some irons in de fire."

"What goes around comes around," the well dressed dude said impassively.

"What's dat?"

"I said, what goes around comes around. You get what your hand calls for."

"Whatcha talking bout?"

"Unless you're thick in the head, you know what I'm talking about. What goes up comes down, don't it? Well, the same principle applies to the big circle. It's like a merry-go-round. You go around, then you come around. It's a universal happening. Everything evens out in the end."

"Oh, I dig it now. I was dealing heavy till I got my nuts caught in de sand."

The well dressed dude scoffed. "Who you trying to impress? You couldn't make a circle big enough to cover an ant hole. How are you going to come around, when you don't even go around?"

Hapless shrugged, silently cursing the plight of the small time hustler, who had to listen to trash like this just to get something to eat.

"Then don't sit there running off at the jibs. You never had nothing to lose and you don't even dig it. You're in good shape compared to the lames on the big wheel, especially when it starts coming back around. The Valley of

Hinnon is drunk with mortgagers who went around and couldn't come around."

"Valley of who? Where's dis valley at?"

"Hee hee hee. . . . Don't worry, baby. When you get there I'll give you the *tour de special.*"

"Suppose I don't want to go to dis valley?"

"Oh, you'll go. There ain't no tricks that can trick the tricker. You got one advantage though."

"What's dat?"

"You been down so long and done got so low, that when you fall you'll get up with your knees skinned a little. When them cats up top fall, there ain't nothing left to get up. I know a million souls, who wished they would've stayed lowly. Take that fool back there. . . ."

"Dat dude on de table?"

"Yup. Would you believe he once had such a melifluous rap that they called him Spiel? Why, there was a time when he could talk the rankness out of pee and sell it for perfume. And women? Man, he had a string of thoroughbreds longer'n the George Washington Bridge."

"You got to be stuffing, man! Look at him!"

"Why would I lie, Hapless? I admit he's in pretty bad shape now, all right. He just sits there in that corner twenty-four hours of every day, pulling his nappy hair, gnashing his teeth and frothing at the mount like a rabid canine. He can't do nothing, see nothing, say nothing. Hee hee hee. . . ."

"What's so funny bout dat?"

"Just a private joke, Hap. Hee hee hee. . . . I been coming to the Table D'hote De Pig every day, just to watch Spiel do his thing. Yes-sir, he is a living witness to the thing that goes around comes around. But he wasn't always that way. He was king of the barnyard, high on the pig's nose, E.S.K."

"What's dat E.S.K.?"

" 'E,' as in epicurean, 'S,' as in swank and 'K,' as in cool. Spiel was one smooth M.F."

"Motherfu. . . . ?"

"Naw, fool, Mickey Flynn."

"How long's he been like dat?"

"Oh, about a year."

"No argument there, but Big Mama won't sign the commitment papers. She says there ain't nobody putting her Spiel in the funny factory."

"Ain't nothing being done for him?"

"Big Mama takes him over to see this little female demonologist in Harlem every Tuesday and gets him some medicine. This week he's on a concoction made out of a Georgia jackrabbit's crushed hind leg muscles, eight ounces of milk from a Caucasus she wolf, two fingers of purified honey, the calcined blood vessels of a baby possum and three heaping teaspoons full of wheat germ."

"Doing any good?"

"Hasn't yet. The little Harlem witch don't know what kind of spell's been cast on Spiel and that mess I just mentioned is supposed to shed some light on the matter. Hey, there's Big Mama now, wiping his nose and giving him his grog. Hee hee hee. . . . Look at the smoke coming out of that glass! Boy, that ought to set his tail on fire."

"Big Mama sure is wide," Hapless speculated out loud.

"No argument there," the well dressed dude said. "Guess that's why she owns this cafe de grease. It's probably the only way she can stock up enough food to keep that frame on the move. She ain't a bad woman though. She made sure Spiel had the chance at an education."

"Did he finish high school?"

"High school? Man, that ain't no education! Spiel went to college and majored in theology, no less. He learned to speak five languages, which included Latin, Greek, French, Spanish and Swahili."

"Did he graduate?"

"Naw, but not because his skull was empty. He got his jelly-snatchers on some ancient manuscripts, that some French dude named Duc de La Vallire had collected and was going around the campus trying to put together one of those cabalistic cults. The college board of directors got wind of what he was doing and tossed him out."

"Sounds like Spiel had a lot on de ball."

"True, but he wasn't even on the pig's nose yet; just another soul brother trying to do his thing. He didn't start executing right, until he got some guidance from the master-doer."

"You keep mentioning Big Mama all de time. What about Spiel's daddy?"

"Snake Pit? Spiel never got a chance to know him. Snake Pit got himself killed by some woman he was back-alleying with. That happened before Spiel could even walk. Big Mama raised him all by her lonesome."

Hapless shook his head sympathetically. "Dat's a damn shame."

"What's so shameful about it? It's what I been telling you all along. Snake Pit got what his hand called for. He went around, then came around."

"Who's dis master doer dat gave Spiel all dis guidance?"

"The well dressed dude looked at his watch. "That's a long story."

"If you got de time, I got it too," Hapless said quickly, fearing that the trick might move out before he could hit him up for some scratch. "I'm gonna sit here as long as I can. It's colder'n a polar bear's buns out dere."

The well dressed dude shrugged. "Well, I guess the beginning would be about three years ago, right after Spiel got canned from college. Keep in mind that Big Mama took the loss of Snake Pit pretty hard and brainwashed Spiel into thinking that the world was full of nothing but treacherous women. When he grew up, it was with an inbred fear of the female species.

"He could converse slick with the fellows, but when it came to rapping with women, he was a blank. Anyway, his hangout buddies started wondering about his manliness, insinuating that he might be gay. After a few busted heads, which only seemed to lend credence to the charges, Spiel decided to do something once and for all about the remarks.

"He still had the Duc's manuscripts stashed away in a closet and figured it was time to find out if the recipe's would really work. For three days he pored over the scripts, straining his eyes, racking his brain, dreaming of the women he would know after he put the thing on them. While studying the parchments he came across a scroll written in Latin. His college learning served him in good stead and at the end of another three days he had finished deciphering the manuscript. It was the ritual for summoning up the *Prince of Players*."

"Satan?"

"Hapless, if your brains wasn't drowning in that twenty-five cent Sterno you been drinking all your life, you would know who I meant. Who else? Now, Spiel re-read the script, making sure he understood everything, then copied down a list of the items he would need. He took the list to a little underground herb shop in The Village and a half hour later was back in his pad with the Satan summoning paraphernalia. He took the stuff into the kitchen and started following the instruction.

"The first item was a stainless steel skillet—he didn't have the type of cauldron specified—and he put this on the stove. When the bottom turned red, he started sprinkling in the various livers, hearts, blood, brains, serpent tongues, gator scales, and other dehydrated ingredients, always calling out the name of a prominent arch demon every time he dropped something into the pan. The last ingredient was an expensive pint of homogenized tarantula milk and when the last drop hit the skillet a cloud of azure vapor rose over the stove.

"Spiel watched the bubbling mess anxiously, because the bubbles signified the efforts of the demons as they pleaded with the prince. If the brew, after it cooled, was smooth and could be smeared on the body like axle grease, it meant that there was a good chance for an interview. But if the mixture turned out like peanut brittle, it meant that Lucifer didn't want to be bothered. Woozy from the smoke, Spiel carried everything into the living room. He put the skillet on the sofa, the softest place he could find, and stripped naked. Next, he made a circle around himself and the sofa, with a vial of dried scorpion blood. Then came a frenzied dance, something like the Funky Broadway, which included some fierce wailing and screaming, similiar to the sound that's coming out of Detroit. . . ."

"Didn't nobody complain bout de noises?"

"Hapless, why don't you rap about something intelligent? People in New York don't care what you do, just as long as you don't do it to them. Now, Spiel completed his contortions and checked the contents of the pan. . . ."

"All dis was done in de middle of de circle?"

"Yeah, stupe, in the circumference of the scorpion blood. Now, Spiel had come to the apex of the ceremony. The batch was pasty and he smeared it all over his body. 'Effeton!' he cried. 'Attas! Canaba! I apply you to implore Lucifer in my behalf! I am his obedient servant! Heli! Heli! Heli!' The room grew warm, then hot, and a cloud of thick red smoke engulfed everything. Slowly the smoke began to clear and when it was gone, there he was, *The Man, The Prince of Hell,* sitting on the sofa with his legs crossed and smoking a reefer the size of a clarinet. . . ."

"Man, Satan don't smoke no pot!"

"He don't smoke pot, huh? Well let me clue you quick, Hapless Jones! He not only smokes pot, but he skin pops too! Where in the heaven do you think vice came from?"

"Dat's hard to believe."

"Strains your credibility, does it? If I said Lucifer was a little red dude with a tail and a pitchfork, you'd buy that. Well, he ain't like that. As a matter of fact, he's tall, refined, good looking and wears a hundred dollar square rigged Afro. On this particular occasion he was bagging a pure white double breasted suit, set off by a purple crepe turtle neck shirt and a one print pair of keen-toed snow-white

33

alligator shoes. The only thing on him that was red was the glowing tip of his king sized reefer."

"Was Spiel scared?"

"He was shook, but he didn't panic. 'What's happening?' he said to Lucifer lightly.

" 'All depends on what you want to happen,' Lucifer replied just as lightly.

" 'That's a mean bag you're bagging,' Spiel said. 'Botany? I go for them stomps too. Bostonian? You are without doubt the hooked up-est dude I have ever seen.'

"Spiel sure knew what to say out of his mouth, because in a minute old Lucifer was telling him about the spiders that spun the material for his suit and his farm, which bred pure stock snow white alligators."

" 'You look like me,' Spiel said, and blew the mood.

" 'Who'd you expect me to look like?' Lucifer asked with a disposition.

"Spiel wanted to shut up, but he didn't know how. 'I always thought Satan was a little . . .' "

" 'Well now you know different,' Lucifer snarled, jabbing his reefer at Spiel. 'Look lame; you interrupted a boss session I was having with Jezebel. We was blowing grass and reciting Persian poetry. I only came up because I ain't been on the turf in a hundred and nine years. And just to set you straight on who looks like who, the priority is mine. Dig it? Now tell me what you want and if I decide to let you have it, I'll quote the price you must pay.'

"So, Spiel told Lucifer about his hang-up with women and about the depreciating remarks the fellows was making about him. He explained sadly that all he wanted to do was enjoy the fruits of the succulent species. He told Lucifer that he was twenty-seven years old and had never known a woman.

" 'Can you do something for me?' Spiel asked pitifully. 'I'm not after fortune, fame or world acclaim. All I want is a chance to show them pseudo cats, who think they know everything, that they don't know nothing.'

"Lucifer was moved to compassion by Spiel's plea. 'You poor soul! You poor miserable soul! To think—not even once! For Beelzebub's sake! It's no wonder you're so discontented. Well, you called for the right stud, Spiel. I am *Thee One, The Seventh Son,* the only true connoiseur of the creature known as woman. I was there first too, my man. If you remember your theology lessons you will recall that it was I who first introduced the art of deception to Eve. Seems like only yesterday. . . .'

" 'Anyway, a lot of cats been using my thing without consulting me, but because you first sought my counsel before attempting anything, I'm going to lend you the bronze tailsman of Aphrodite. Whenever it is around your neck you will be receiving the direct current of my influence. No woman will be able to resist your powerful thing.'

"Lucifer made a sign with his hand and there appeared in the room the loveliest, most licentuous, creature Spiel had ever seen. She wore a hip-hugging mini, with a purple sash knotted up high under her majestic breasts and kicked a pair of snow white alligator pumps. In her two hands she held a blood-red velvet pillow, and nestling in the center of it was the bronze medal of Aphrodite, with the signs of the seven planets engraved on both sides. She held the pillow out to Lucifer.

" 'Hi, Lukey. Is this what you wanted?'

35

" 'Yeah, mama,' the Prince of Hell replied, and slapped her smartly on her heart-shaped rump. 'Bel, I want you to meet my man Spiel. You'll have to excuse his appearance. He wasn't expecting company. Don't be shy, Spiel. Bel knows what's happening.'

" 'Hi Stuff,' Jezebel said to Spiel. 'What's uptown?'

"As was his custom in the presence of bewitching women, Spiel could only gape, and try to cover his nakedness.

" 'I can't use your inexperienced soul right now, Spiel,' Lucifer said, getting back down to business, 'because I got some dudes operating now that would make you look like an Alabama cotton picker at the Newport Jazz Festival. So, what I'm gonna do is lend you the talisman free of charge. Later, after you acquire some polish and, if you aspire to even greater heights, we'll talk about a soul deal. Okay?'

"Spiel got off a nod, but he was concerned only with Jezebel's captivating beauty.

"Lucifer dug it and laughed. 'There is only one stipulation, which necessity seems to dictate since your goggles have been constantly exploring my woman's asphasiac loveliness, and that is you should not attempt to summon or communicate with Jezebel. She is mine, exclusively, and to paraphrase an expression employed by my chief rival: "My tail is long and my retribution total." Spiel, for such an affront to my personal dignity, after my patronism of you, I would reduce you to the state of a babbling idiot. Do you understand?'

"Spiel managed another nod, but his eyes continued to devour the voluptuous Jezebel.

"Lucifer stood up and put the talisman around Spiel's neck. 'Remember the condition,' he warned. 'Come on, tramp!' he snapped at Jezebel, and started fading from view behind a wall of fire red smoke.

" 'I'm coming daddy,' Jezebel called, giving Spiel's glistening black body a last meaningful inspection. 'You can send for me, baby,' she whispered hurriedly. 'Use the same ritual, but leave out Lukey and the demons. They ain't nothing but his stool pigeons. Goodbye, baby. . . .'

" 'Not goodbye!' Spiel cried after the dissolving enchantress. 'Never say goodbye!' "

"Is dat how Spiel fell?" Hapless cut in.

"Be cool," the well dressed dude said impatiently. "I'm coming to it. . . . Spiel moved into a split level pad on Park Avenue South. Man, that crib was laid out. He had wall-to-wall carpeting three inches thick, a stereo unit with upteen speakers and a bar that was stocked with everything from canned heat to pink champagne. . . ."

"Didn't nobody complain bout a black man up dere in dat neighborhood?"

"Naw. They thought Spiel was a fashion model. He already had the gift of gab. Add the power of the talisman and you can well understand why the white folks didn't raise a ruckus. You should've seen those top shelf broads pursuing him, and he changed them like he changed his shorts, twice a day. And speaking of clothes . . . a lame like you couldn't even pronounce the names on the tags in his rags. He wore doublebreasted acetate and overcoats made out of chinchilla and saber paws. . . ."

"Saber paws?"

"Yeah, saber paws. They come from the Ural Mountains in Russia." The well dressed dude stopped and gave Hapless a long penetrating stare. "Anything else you want to know, like rain is wet, grass is green, bulls snort and polar bears have hair, or do you want me to finish?"

"Go head."

"Well, Spiel drove an olive-green Dushenberg, complete with telephone, hi-fi, television and power everything. Then he messed it all up. . . ."

"What'd he do?"

"He summoned Jezebel."

"Did he cop?"

"He not only copped, but he planted a human seed in Bel. When Lucifer got the news he was fit to be tied. That dude back there in the corner, assuming that pre-historic position, is the result of Lucifer's wrath."

"And dat's how come Spiel's like he is?"

"That's it."

"How come you is sitting here watching him? You a freak for digging other cats misery?"

"Hap, the answer to that will really strain your brain.

"I'm listening."

"I come to watch Spiel do his thing because I'm the dude that put the thing on him. Also, I come to make sure that little root worker don't pull the spell up off his back. She been mixing up some potent stuff."

"You saying dat you is Satan?"

"I am *he*," the well dressed dude said solemnly.

Hapless doubted if he could stand too much more of this cat's lying, so he moved right into the Jeff Game. "Well, since you is de devil, you sure nuff got to be a good doing cat and it won't be nothing for you to conjure me up a quarter, so I can get me an entree of Big Mama's chitterlings and crackling bread. I'm hungry'n a wildcat fresh off a piece of tail."

The man who claimed he was Satan shook his head sadly. "Hap, I got to tell you like it is. I got problems, heavy ones, and if I had a quarter to spare I'd gladly give it to you. The fact of the matter is, I ain't. I just had a new electrical unit installed in my Hadey Lake Villa, Plus I had to buy Bel a jet plane to make up for the loss of Spiel. My arch-demons threatened a walk-out unless I bought them some anti-diathermal underwear and that alone put me on E Street and Zero Avenue. And if that ain't enough, I can't look old man Hippocrates in the eye because I ain't got the coin to pay him for the abortion he done on Bel or for treating the victims of the Hong Kong epidemic that struck my Fire Valley Province last week. To top everything off, just the other night a sulphur storm hit Gehenna and I got to pay Canaba fives cents a head for transporting the destitute souls to Tartarus. To make matters even worse, I ain't got no wheels. Rudamount borrowed my Styxmobile, got high off a pint of gunghy and crashed into one of my soul crematoriums. I ain't got carfare to welfare, not to mention giving you a quarter."

Haples wrinkled his face distastefully. "I been sitting here for two hours, listening to you spew all them lies out of your face, and now you tell me you ain't got a quarter. If you're the devil, then I'm King Kong. In fact, I ought to smack you right in the chops."

The well dressed dude held up a hand. "No reason to affect an attitude, Hap," he said, unruffled. "You ain't the only one in bad shape. Whenever you feel a draft through that raggedy coat or look down and see them holey sneakers, just think about the dudes that ain't even got that. You'll be surprised how vivified you'll feel. Now, as for puting your paws in my reverend jibs—don't! We'd both end up in the hospital, you to get your butt sewed up and me to get my foot out!"

"You jive mother . . ."

"Hold it right there, Hap. That may be true in some cases, but not yours. Your mama was uglier'n a bowl of yakamane. And while I'm at it, what happened to all them de's and dat's? I knew you was shukking when you came in the door. That's why your tail don't fit in the circle—it's too square."

The well dressed dude stood up and slid into a luxurious green fur overcoat.

"What's that coat made out of?" Hapless snickered. Green rat fur? And how come you know my name?"

The man who called himself Lucifer grinned. "Dis coat was made in de Valley of Hinnon. Dat's where I keep my ranch dat breeds grass green grizzly bears. De answer to question numeral deuce is—I know all fools! *Laterus lamus!* Don't get no ideas! Your brain might explode!"

Hapless blinked twice as the well dressed dude disappeared in a puff of fire red smoke.

RUBIN (HURRICANE) CARTER
#45742

Rubin, once a top contender for the middleweight boxing title, is presently serving a ridiculous sentence of triple life. He spends most of his time preparing legal briefs for presentation in the various courts and working on his autobiography, The Sixteenth Round, *which is soon to be published by Viking Press. When asked to write down a few things about himself, he replied this way: "What can I say? I'm 35 years old, good looking, and haven't been kissed in six years. My thing is hunting, horses, and my family."*

RETURN OF THE KID

by

Rubin (Hurricane) Carter

MANNY THOMAS PURSED HIS LIPS THOUGHT-
fully. "I think you need some new faces. Even boxing fans
aren't dumb enough to believe Keegan can win every week.
He's damn near forty years old."

Charlie Wildcat Higgins puffed furiously on the stub
of a bent up cigar. "Yeah, but how can you tell what a
fight fan thinks? If he thinks at all." He had been a middleweight boxer before turning promoter and hadn't made
much money at either profession, but matching fighters
once a week was a lot better than getting slammed all over
the arena.

"I gave up trying to figure out fight fans after the first
Liston-Clay bout," Manny said. He was publicity agent for
Charles Higgins Promotions, Incorporated, a slender young
man with dark hair, blue eyes and a lazy manner. "I do

know the gate at the Sports Palace has been dropping every week. Why don't you bring in some new faces?"

Charlie absently stroked one of his cauliflowered ears. "I still got Lefty Matthews," he said defensively.

"Lefty's the opposite of Keegan," Many scoffed. "Even the kids are starting to wonder why he can't win a bout."

Charlie propped his feet on his desk, which was as worn and battered as he was. "If Lefty won a bout, he wouldn't draw flies, unless he jumped in a garbage can before each fight."

"You better come up with something," Manny warned. "At this rate, you'll be out of business in three months."

"There ain't nothing to come up with!" Charlie exclaimed. He threw up his hands in frustration. "I had family night, kid's night, ladies night. . . . I even gave out miniature boxing gloves. . . ." He caught himself and glowered at Manny. "Whatta you mean I gotta come up with sump'n? You get seventy-five smacks a week for handling the publicity."

Manny dropped into a rickety straight-backed chair in front of Charlie's desk. "You're right," he soothed. "I'll figure out something."

"I'm all ears."

"I can see that," Manny commented dryly.

Charlie was touchy about his ears. They were his proudest features and he'd be damned if he'd let a skinny little snip like Manny make cracks about them. "Whatta you mean, wiseacre? I got these ears from mixing it with some of the ring's greatest: Cerdan, Zale, Rocky, Sugar. . . . Man, that Sugar had a left hook that was a blur. Half the time you couldn't even see it. . . ."

44

Manny jumped up so violently that he turned over his chair. "That's it! That's it!"

"What's it?" Charlie looked at his publicity agent like he'd gone crazy.

"The Invisible Kid!" Manny exclaimed.

Charlie snorted through the nostrils of his twisted nose. "You trying to razz me? I ain't never heard of no Invisible Kid."

Manny pointed to a vacant corner. "He's right over there!"

Charlie looked. "I don't see nobody."

"He's invisible," Manny said. "You can't see somebody who's invisible."

Charlie made a face. "You just got done telling me about how the fans ain't dumb enough to keep buying Kayo Keegan every Friday night, now you're trying to tell me they're stupid enough to go for this Invisible Kid brainstorm of yours. If he ain't there, he ain't there!"

"You need something different," Manny insisted.

"What you're talking about sure is different," the promoter said caustically.

But Manny was inflamed with the idea. "Look, we match Kayo with the Invisible Kid. Kayo promises publicly to hang up his gloves if he loses. When he gets bombed out the fans'll go wild."

"And so will the State Athletic Commission," Charlie put in. "We'll both end up in the slammers."

"Come on," Manny reasoned. "The State Athletic Commission never even heard of Millville. You got Keegan billed as the only living middleweight with ninety-seven fights and ninety-seven victories, and he isn't even rated in the *Millville Republican.*"

"Suppose we pulled it off?" Charlie asked. "What happens to Kayo?"

Manny had that figured too. "We put a mask on him. He'll have a brand new start, five or ten more years."

Charlie chewed on his cigar stub. "I don't know. . . . When I was in my prime we didn't need any tricks to pack 'em in. Hell, Sugar had a left-hook that . . ."

". . . was a blur," Manny finished for him.

Charlie was still skeptical. "If my brains was scrambled eggs, you couldn't make me believe there was somebody in that corner."

"How can you expect to see somebody who's invisible?" Manny asked.

Charlie shrugged.

"We get Keegan in here for a meeting and we tell him like it is," Manny pressed, one idea feeding the other. "We tell him that he's not pulling in the fans anymore, that he's got to meet the Invisible Kid and take a dive. . . ."

"What about marks?" Charlie wanted to know. "How's it gonna look if he hits the apron and there ain't even a scratch on his face?"

"We get some red dye," Manny countered easily. "We tape it on his wrist, right under the laces, and we use a thin plastic pack so it'll break when he rubs it across his face. You'll be in his corner and you can tell him what he's doing wrong."

"Where'll you be at?" Charlie asked suspiciously.

Manny laughed, reading the promoter's thoughts. "I'll be in the Invisible Kid's corner."

"Doing what?"

"Rubbing him down and giving him instructions," Manny replied.

Charlie managed another miraculous puff on his cigar stub and crushed it out in a sardine can on his desk. He blew out a cloud of hazy blue smoke and squinted through it. "I still don't see how Kayo can fight somebody that don't exist."

"But he will exist!" Manny exclaimed. "If everybody does their part, the Invisible Kid will be as real as you and me."

Charlie hesitated a moment longer, then made a decision and his battered face lit up in a grin. "Maybe you got sump'n. It's just wacky enough to work."

On Thursday, Kayo Keegan walked into Charlie's office. He was a likeable brute, with not too much in the intelligence department. He was quite surprised at the arrangements that had been made for him, but to the amazement of both the promoter and the publicity agent he readily agreed. He especially liked the idea of a mask later on. Maybe they could call him the Masked Bomber or the Mystery Kid.

The two schemers spent the remainder of the day promoting and publicizing. Manny had posters printed and put them up everywhere but in the city jail, while Charlie took out a full-page ad in the *Millville Republican* and bought twelve, one-minute commercials from WMLV, the local radio station.

Friday night, the Millville Sports Palace—a converted airplane hanger on the outskirts of town—was filled to overflowing. Many fans had to be turned away at the door; but for the fortunate ones who got inside, they were treated to a sight never before equaled in ring history. In one corner, Charlie Higgins worked furiously around Kayo Keegan, while on the opposite side of the ring, Manny Thomas was doubly active. But, if there was anyone else there he certainly was invisible.

Johnny Addle, three days older than air and twice as polluted, waited for the arena to fill and hobbled to the center of the ring. "Ladieeeeeeeees and gentlemeeeeeeeeen! Because of the enormous amount of preparation in getting ready for tonight's monumental action, we are going to forego the usual string of preliminaries and get right down to the nitty gritty."

He let the appreciative titter make its rounds of the auditorium before continuing. "In the corner on my left . . . weighing one hundred and sixty-five pounds and three-quarters . . . winner of ninety-seven fights without a defeat . . . sixty-nine via the kayo route . . . wearing the white trunks with the black stripe running down the side . . . Milville's own . . . Kayo Keeeeeeeeeegaaaaaaaaaan!"

A thunderous applause shook the old building. Johnny Addle shuffled cards importantly, even though there were only two. "His opponent . . . in the corner on my right . . . weighing in at one hundred and sixty-eight pounds even . . . winner of fifty-four bouts without a loss . . . all by knockouts . . . returning to the ring after five years of retirement . . . wearing the invisible trunks with the invisible stripe running down the side . . . from the East Indian island of Sakoa . . . the Invisible Kiiiiiiiiiid!"

An icy silence greeted the fighter nobody could see. All the fans could do was stare, blink their eyes, and try to peer through the cloak of invisibility.

Jersey Jack Willcut, five minutes older than shoe leather and two shades darker, called the contestants to the center of the ring for their instructions. Every eye was on Manny Thomas, who whispered in his fighter's ear, while his arm seemed to be draped in mid-air. A moment later the gladiators and their trainers returned to their respective corners. At the twenty-second warning buzzer Manny and Charlie pulled the stools out of the ring.

Kayo was already moving to the center of the canvas when the bell sounded. The crowd applauded when he stuck out two crisp jabs and went into the Keegan shuffle. A double left hook combination, topped off with a straight right hand, brought the fans out of their seats. It was obvious that Kayo was taking charge early.

The second round went on in much the same manner, with Kayo having an easy time of it, showing everything in his repertoire. But near the end of the round he gave ground and his head snapped back several times, as if receiving a flurry of short stabs in the mouth.

Between rounds Charlie rinsed off Kayo's mouthpiece. "You're doing beautiful," he whispered in the fighter's ear, but just before the warning buzzer he noticed a befuddled expression on Kayo's face. He figured it was time to end it. No sense pushing a good thing too far. "Now!" he hissed at Kayo, and pulled the stool out of the ring.

Kayo danced out, but the lightness was gone from his toes and after a few steps he gave up the Keegan Shuffle.

49

He tried a jab, but it appeared feeble and ineffective, almost like a goodbye wave to a dear friend. He started a left hook, pulled it back, then whipped it out uncertainly again. He wound up rabbit punching himself alongside the ear.

Then suddenly an invisible haymaker spun his head sideways. He stumbled, recovered, and backpedaled furiously. An imperceptible sledge hammer caught up with him, dug into his mid-section and slammed him back against the ropes. He bounced off the ropes, crouched low, arms across his face peek-a-boo style. An unseen uppercut drove through his guard and lifted him to his toes. When his heels touched the canvas, he kept sliding right on down, like a puppet whose strings had been cut.

A dazed hush engulfed the auditorium. Even those who were a part of the hoax gaped goggle-eyed: Johnny Addle kept blinking his eyes; Jersey Jack stood scratching the side of his head and forgot the countout; but there were no sounds of derision. Charlie Higgins was hardly noticed as he helped Kayo Keegan through the ropes.

Johnny Addle recovered first and hobbled to the center of the ring, arms upraised for quiet. It was unnecessary because silence already reigned supreme in the Millville Sports Palace. "Ladieeeeeeeeees and gentlemeeeeeeeeeen! The winner . . . by a knockout . . . in . . ."—Johnny squinted at a huge clock held up by Judge Lambist, who was four days older than icebergs and five degrees colder—". . . thirty-four seconds of the third round . . . the Invisible Kiiiiiiiiiid!"

The silence gave way to pandemonium, rising and falling waves of applause, accolades for the fighter nobody could see. Manny shouldered a path to the dressing room, as fans poured into the aisles, reaching out, straining for a touch of the Invisible Kid. At the door of the arena's single dressing room Manny slapped the invisible fighter on the butt.

"Okay, champ! Let's hit the shower." Manny closed the door and leaned against it, face aglow with glee. "Hot damn!" he shouted. "How's that for an idea?"

Charlie had Kayo down on the rubdown table. He chuckled. Outside, the crowd still thundered its approval. "Okay, Kayo, let's unlace those gloves. After you wash that gook off, we'll put on some bandages for show."

Kayo struggled to a sitting position and Charlie took a good look at his face. One whole cheek was swollen blue and there were crimson welts on his neck. A huge purple lump completely closed one eye.

"How'd you manage that?" Manny asked, coming off the door. Kayo groaned something unintelligible.

"Kayo, you missed your calling," Charlie bubbled, pulling off the boxing gloves. "You should've been a movie . . ." His mouth clamped suddenly shut and his breath came in one long gulp. He glanced quickly at Manny, who was staring at Kayo's wrist and the little packet of red dye still taped in place. Though both of them saw, neither believed, until the water started running in the shower stall.

51

WILLIAM (WILLIE) SELPH
#36512

Willie immigrated to the New Jersey Prison System from Newark's south side, and brought 65 years with him. A more personable individual you couldn't find and his ready smiles and jokes are a constant source of amazement, considering the burden he carries. Even the most pessimistic of persons would find it difficult to dislike him.

THE MIRACLE WORKER

by

William (Willie) Selph

A FINE MIST FELL SOFTLY ON THE CIRCUS-LIKE
revival tent and shimmered in a lonely stream of light that
was filtering through a slit in the front flap; but to the people inside—600 of them, white, brown, black—the damp
evening was a thing of little account. They writhed and
moaned and laughed, in time to an open-shirted gospel
hymn that was being pounded out by an organ, drum, and
piano combo. On the dying chords of "My Redeemer,"
Reverend B. B. Bootaker bounced onto the stage, resplen-
dant in a blood-red silk suit. The crowd knew him as God's
Man of Faith and Power.

"Sisters and brothers," he began in a deep Ozark bari-
tone, "when ever people ask me what I think witnessing
for the Lord is, they always ask the question like there's a
big secret to it. Well, I want to tell you here and now,

there is no secret. Being a witness for the Lord is simply knowing Him. Being a witness for the Lord is simply loving Him. Being a witness for the Lord is simply serving Him. Being a witness for the Lord is helping pay to send His message all around the world. You got to vow and pay. You got to promise God and you got to keep your promise. There is no place in heaven for earthly possessions, neither is there a place in heaven for liars."

At that moment two attendants wheeled in an ambulance stretcher, carrying a black woman, totally wrapped in bandages. "This is a sad story," B. B. said solemnly. "This woman was admitted to the hospital yesterday, with third degree burns all over her body. She'd been home, high on dope, when her clothes caught fire in the kitchen." B. B. bent over the victim. "Do you believe God can raise you up?"

"Yes. . . . Yes . . . ," the woman replied weakly, evincing great pain.

"Then the cure is halfway completed, because your soul is already cleansed." B. B. nodded and the attendants trundled the stretcher behind a wide screen. "Raise your hands in prayer," B. B. commanded the crowd, and twelve hundred hands reached for the roof. In the back, a raisin-faced woman on crutches caressed her Bible.

"Please, sweet Jesus," she whimpered.

Some of the worshippers heard and picked up the cry, "Please, sweet Jesus."

"Heal this woman!" B. B. shouted.

"Heal!" the crowd chanted.

"Please, sweet Jesus!" B. B. yelled.

"Please, sweet Jesus!" the throng echoed.

Suddenly the black woman rushed around the screen, pulling off the last of her bandages. "It's a miracle!" she announced, tears of joy and mystification streaming down her cheeks. "There is new skin covering the burns!" She knelt at B. B.'s feet and began kissing the hem of his red silk pants.

The combo struck up a hymn and there was singing and dancing and clapping. Brother Arnold Walsh, shaped like an ebony pear, waddled down the aisle taking names, addresses and pledges. Before the hymn ended he was back on stage with God's Man of Faith and Power, who stood tall and smiling. The combo banged out a few more chords and trailed off. B. B. glanced at the list of pledges and his smile was radiant.

"Thank you brothers and sisters. Whomsoever gives without limit, him shall the Lord repay tenfold in heaven. All man needs is to be in the center of God's . . ."

"Please help me!" came a desperate croaking voice. "Please. . . ." The little raisin-faced woman came down the aisle on crutches, aided by a thin man wearing horn rimmed glasses.

Brother Walsh recognized instantly the worst dread of a faith healer, the truly maimed. He blocked the path to the stage with his ponderous frame. "I am genuinely sorry," he said in a grieved tone. "Reverend Bootaker has drawn an enormous amount of power from the Lord today."

The thin man tried to turn the old woman around. "Come on, Mithuth Thmith," he said testily. "I told you thith thtuff wath for the birdth."

The old lady resisted. "He can heal me!" she rasped.

"Heal her!" the crowd clamored. "She believes!"

Perhaps it was the roar of the six hundred voices, perhaps it was the naked plea in the old crone's wrinkled face. Whatever, B. B. decided to heal her. "Let them pass, Brother Walsh."

B. B.'s top pledge-getter glanced quickly at his boss, but the serene smugness of B. B.'s smile allayed his fears. He chuckled inwardly. The old hijacker must have arranged this one himself. He helped the old woman onto the stage.

B. B. looked at her closely, his face a show of deep compassion. "How did you become ill, my child?"

"A car accident . . . ," the woman sobbed. "Twenty years ago. . . ."

The man wearing the horn rimmed glasses stood just to one side of the crippled old lady. B. B. spoke to him. "And you . . . of little faith. Were you born with a lisp?"

"How the hell elth do you get a lithp?" the tongue tied man retorted.

Reverend Bootaker sighed. "Profanity doesn't help your cause any."

"Neither doth all thith blabbing."

"If I cured you of your lisp," B. B. asked, "would such a thing bring you into the house of the Lord?"

The thin man laughed sarcastically. "Baby, thuch a thing would bwing me through hell with gatholine drawerth on!"

"What is your name?" B. B. asked.

The tongue tied man hesitated. "Ith Thomath Roth. That'th with a double eth."

"And yours?"

"Myra Smith, the old lady whimpered.

B. B. nodded. "All right, Mr. Ross. Will you help Mrs. Smith behind the screen?"

Mr. Ross shrugged. "Ith worth a twy."

After they disappeared behind the screen, B. B. turned to his flock. "Everybody raise your hands towards heaven and clench your fists. We need to draw double power from the Lord this time." He closed his eyes and looked upward, his face a show of deep concentration. "Jesus, we have two tragedies here, a good woman struck down in a car accident and a lost sinner with a terrible lisp. Show us Thy power! Show us Thy mercy!"

"Power!" the multitude clamored.

"Heal this God fearing woman!" B. B. bellowed.

"Mercy!" the mass trumpeted.

"Heal this unbeliever also!" B. B. screamed.

"Heal!" the assemblage urged.

"Mrs. Smith!" B. B. shouted above the din.

"Yes . . . ? Yes . . . ?

"Throw away your crutches!" B. B. commanded.

Both of the old lady's crutches sailed over the screen and the noise died to an awed whisper. Even B. B. Bootaker gasped. "Mr. Ross! Tell us what miracles the Lord has wrought!"

The silence itself was deafening and even the rain pattering on the canvas roof seemed as if it had stopped to listen. When Mr. Ross spoke his voice was heard in every corner of the tent.

"No miwacle. Mithuth Thmith juth fell on her ath."

FRANK EARL ANDREWS
#40030

Frank is 31 years old and a product of Millville, New Jersey. Having spent most of his life under supervision of some sort, he was categorized by one small town judge, as a symbol of this country's defective correctional system. After the judge made this monumental speech, he bound Frank over to the state for 67 years of rehabilitation.

Frank has sold material to Event, Liberty, Accent on Youth, *and a few others. Though the credits may not seem impressive to some, he is immensely proud of his accomplishments, considering the circumstances. He is currently working on an account of his life:* The Diary of a Convict—My First One Thousand Years.

YNNEL EHT NAITRAM

by

Frank Earl Andrews

TALL PAUL FOUND HIS OLD LADY IN THE EXIST-
ence room, peeping out into the rear yard. He gleamed
over her scapula and dug Little Paul, practicing karate and
giggling, in front of a miniature playpad that was damn
near blocked off by the tangled branches of a teeny Mac-
Intosh tree.

"Getting off on his lonesome again," Big Bertha snitched
to her old man. "He won't kick with the other brats. I don't
think that kid's wrapped too tight."

She had her mandibles propped open to transmit something else, but Little Paul cruised in. The facade of his
pentad year-old head was heart shaped, spherical at the
chin and ruled by an army of freckles. He beeped his pro-
genitors a cursory greeting.

"Well, what has my diminutive tiger been up to this post
meridiem?" Tall Paul queried.

"Zero," Little Paul muttered.

"Discontent is the bastard of idleness," Tall Paul philosophized briskly.

"He gamboled," Big Bertha put in placidly.

Little Paul translocuted his pins. "A little . . ."

"He soloed again," Big Bertha went on. "He doesn't dig other kids."

"He has a right to cull his own sidekicks," Tall Paul justified.

"But he doesn't select any cohorts!" Big Bertha expostulated.

"Incorrect," Little Paul pronounced flocculently.

Big Bertha erected an oculis brow. "Ohhh . . . , who is your confrere?"

"You can't behold him."

"What is his moniker?" Tall Paul craved to cognize.

Little Paul balked.

"Certainly you can trust us," Tall Paul inspirited.

"Lenny . . . ," Little Paul vocalized terminally.

"There is no one toponymed Lenny," Big Bertha scoffed. "It is someone he constructed."

"I didn't make anything up!" Little Paul bleated.

Big Bertha soughed. "Now he's fabricating, and he is being rowdy by elevating his voice. I think we should rap on a different theme."

"Nix, we won't gab about something else!" Tall Paul vociferated firmly. "Punks Little Paul's age take brain trips every day. The thing to do now is demonstrate to him that this Lenny dude is a figment of his own enterprise. Isn't that right, Little Paul? You composed this cat in your mind?"

Little Paul remained obstinate. "Nayfous."

"You did," Tall Paul insisted," and there is no detriment in histrionics; but you must learn to recognize what is naturalistic and what is not. Now, ventilate about this crony of yours and I will display your blooper to you. What does he look like?"

"He's short and fat . . . , most of the time."

"What do you mean by, most of the time?"

"Sometimes he's short and fat; sometimes he makes himself tall and skinny, like a beanpole."

"You're not fearful when he rotates into a beanpole?"

Little Paul chortled. "Negative."

"Well, I'm blissful that he doesn't intimidate you," Tall Paul expressed vocally. "Does he romp on the turf with you?"

"Aye."

"What does he cogitate about you?"

"He digs me and perpetually makes me bust my sides."

"What does he contemplate about your old lady and me?"

Little Paul faltered.

"Proceed," Tall Paul phonated. "Honesty is the brethren of courage."

"He thinks you're a duo of jerk-offs."

Tall Paul counterchanged peeks with Big Bertha. "Why is it that we cannot view him?"

"He doesn't want you to."

Tall Paul shook his noggin fatiguely. "Where did Lenny derive from?"

"The Red Planet."

"Where is his vessel? Is that imperceptible too?"

Little Paul inclined his dome.

"If this Lenny dude is real, why . . ."

Little Paul yowled out abrupty. "Lenny is valid! He is!"

Tall Paul took a buried breath, snooped at the roof, then plunged in anew. "When you hit the back quadrangle is anyone there?"

"Nein."

"Then you deliberate on your comate and he remigrates?"

"I have to rap a special phrase first."

"Whuzzat?"

"Ynnel eht naitram."

Tall Paul effected a disposition. "That is nothing but garbel! It is phoney, just like your chum is!"

"Lenny is bonafide," Little Paul uttered demulcently.

Tall Paul tallied slowly to a dime. When he rapped again his transmission was two octaves lower. "All right, booger, I will show you just how tangible Lenny is. Go into the yard and subpoena him."

"At this juncture."

"This instant. I will be along in a sixetieth of an hour. Tell this creep I want to rap with him, and that I also want to witness him."

"You're not plotting to clobber Little Paul?" Big Bertha interjected.

Little Paul was by the exit, but he picked up Big Bertha's dubietive and stalled. "Lenny won't let anyone injure me," he piped. "He said if anyone endeavored to wallop me, he would have them rapping backwards—from now on!"

Tall Paul faked a left hook at his offspring, livid with rage at his insubordination. "If you don't have enough marbles to climb off of that cloud, after I show you it is only

63

smoke," Tall Paul snarled, "you will indubitably grasp reality when I stick my foot in your little fundament! Now, carry your butt out on the turf!"

After Little Paul left, no one yakked about anything. Big Bertha plopped down in a commodious chair, penitent of the fact that she'd ratted on her male descendant. Tall Paul bided a twinkling and then went outward. A short term subsequent, a terrified screech sliced through the tardy p.m. atmosphere.

Big Bertha leaped to her wheels and hustled for the yard. She was well nigh to the playpad, when she came upon Tall Paul, on his knobbles and clinging desperately to the gnarled trunk of the brief MacIntosh. He looked up at her, but with lamps that comprehended nought.

"Dog mnad!" he blared. "S'eh lear! Ynnel eht naitram! Eh si lear!"

BUSHWHACKED

by

Frank Earl Andrews

JOHNNY CALADIN LAY ON HIS SIDE, FULLY clothed, watching an orange sun fade slowly behind the hills to the west. Nervously, he bit at his lower lip and listened to the noise of the woman in the next room as she cleared off the dinner table.

Later, when there were no more sounds, he swung his legs over the side of the bed and pulled on his boots. For a moment he considered telling her what he meant to do, but cast the idea aside immediately. She wouldn't understand. She hadn't before.

He walked across the room to a large oval mirror on the wall. The face that gazed back at him was a young one, thin, smooth, with a hint of pouting at the lips. The eyes were clear, deep blue, accentuated by sandy colored hair

and eyebrows. The chin was pointed and proud, the cheekbones high, the nose not quite aquiline. He turned his attention to a brown dresser nearby and a nickel plated star. He
looked at it with something akin to reverence, then pinned
it to his shirt.

On a straight-backed chair next to the dresser hung a
wide black metal studded gunbelt. With quick movements
he buckled the belt around his waist, hitched it a few times
to make sure it rode comfortably on his lean hips, then
secured the holster to his thigh with a leather thong. He
walked around the room, making sure everything felt just
right, then put on his Stetson and strode purposefully to the
door. A moment later he was in the street, squinting as the
setting sun glinted off the star on his shirt.

Another figure materialized instantly from between two
houses a few doors down. He was dressed in black, all
black, except for two white gun butts that jutted out from
each hip. He wore a short brimmed hat and had a habit of
tugging at it every few minutes. He too was young, though
he stood a few inches taller than Johnny, and the grin he
wore lit up his smooth cinnamon-colored face.

Johnny took a deep breath and moved forward, placing
one foot directly in front of the other, letting the fingers of
his right hand brush his low slung holster with each step.
The brown youth moved to meet him and when only fifteen
feet separated them, they stopped and glared coldly at one
another.

"See you showed up," the figure in black said.

"Appears that way, Willy," Johnny replied in an exag-
gerated drawl.

66

Willy tugged at his hat brim. "Didn't think you'd show," he said casually.

Johnny didn't say any more. The need for words was past and it was time for action. He went into a deep crouch, keeping his eyes riveted to Willy's. They would tell him. The eyes always told him.

They tensed, muscles tightening for the draw. There was a leaden like silence. Hands were rock steady, lips clamped tight, breathing slow and even.

It seemed an eternity before Johnny saw what he was looking for, just a fluttering of the eyelashes, and in the space of a heartbeat his hand flashed down and up. Too late he realized that Willy had him beat and he saw the white handled guns buck slightly in the brown hands, heard the sharp simultaneous reports, saw the smoke curling from the ends of the barrels.

He took a step backwards, mouth agape, eyes wide in surprise. He hadn't even cleared leather. Willy Mason's lips curved upward into a triumphant grin. Suddenly the smile disappeared and Johnny saw that Willy was looking past, rather than at him. There was someone at his rear.

He whirled, bringing his half holstered gun up in the same motion. It was slapped from his hand. He opened his mouth to speak, but the words caught in his throat and all he could manage was a squeak. "I was just . . ." He jumped forward, just in time to avoid a swipe at the seat of his pants.

"Johnny Caladin!" his mother hissed angrily, bending to pick up his cap pistol. "You march right back into that house! And if you aren't in bed by the time I get there, you're going to get the licking of your life! How many

67

times must I tell you about sneaking out of the house and playing with that colored boy?"

For a moment Johnny didn't move, meaning to defy his mother, meaning to tell her that Willy Mason was a lot of fun, that it didn't matter if his skin was a different color, but his courage seeped out like water through a sieve and he ran for home.

As he fumbled frantically with the doorknob, he glanced over his shoulder and saw Willy, standing alone, with two glittering wet diamonds starting the desolate slide down his russet cheeks.

"We was bushwhacked, Willy!" he cried in a cracked voice. He caught a glimpse of his mother coming up. "Just like being shot in the back," he mumbled, and scooted inside.

WILLIAM (SHOE WILLIE) EDWARDS
#46327

Shoe Willie was born in Washington, D.C., during the Great Depression. At the age of 16 he left home and hustled his way north to Newark, New Jersey. In 1951 Uncle Sam caught up with him and sent him to Korea, where he served with the 101st Airborne. On leave to Tokyo he had his first taste of "H" and in 1954 he returned to the U.S. with V.D. and a habit. His current interests are, law work, football and Nancy Wilson.

FIRST CASE FOR CHARLIE

by

William (Shoe Willie) Edwards

IT STARTED LAST FRIDAY, ABOUT TWO IN THE afternoon. I had my feet on the desk, taking all the time in the world assembling and reassembling my .38, which I always did when I had nothing to do, which I had been doing for three weeks, since the inception of Charles Johnson & Associates. The "associates" was just for show. Shit! There wasn't room in that cubby hole for me, let alone any partners. Add the fact that I hadn't seen a soul in days, not even the rent collector, and you can well understand my surprise when a heavy knock rattled my door. I let the hammer down on "Old Equalizer" and dropped it into a drawer.

"It's open," I said, hoping I sounded like Joe Mannix.

The door swung wide and for a minute I didn't think it was wide enough, but the three hundred plus pounds of blubber somehow squeezed his way through. I didn't laugh at the double breasted nightmare he had on, nor the spats, but I did hold my breath when he plopped his ponderous self into my only client's chair. The sorry excuse for a seat had more strength than sense and only emitted a few squeaks. Fatty didn't waste any time and slapped a crisp packet of twenties on my desk. I couldn't remember when green looked better, so I graced him with my best Uncle Tom grin.

"Who do you want killed?"

Fatty missed the humor of my pun and fashioned his plump jaws into an expression of distaste. I didn't know if he disliked the cruddy quarters or the texture of my skin, but I was down to coffee and donut money and Philadelphia's newest black private sleuth needed some work.

"Don't judge a book by its cover, Mister ahhh . . ."

". . . Smith," he wheezed, sounding like a rusty Brillo pad scraping the sides of a frying pan.

I had eyes only for the green. "What do I have to do for that?"

"Solve a murder."

It figured, no simple divorce action for Charles Johnson on his first case. I had to start off with a homicide. Getting back to business, I asked Fatty why he didn't go to the police. I didn't think he could look any uglier, but he frowned and two layers of meat wrinkled around the slits that served as his eyes.

"The Whartonville Police have already investigated the murder," Baby Huey said. "Their books are closed."

"Where's Whartonville?" I asked.

"Mecklenberg County," he answered.

"Where's Mecklenberg County?" I queried, wondering if Fatty was intending to make me ask sixty-four questions before he told me what planet Whartonville was on.

"Virginia."

Now, I knew where Virginia was and I also knew what happened to niggers who went down there nibshitting. I asked Fatty why he came all the way to Philly and what he expected me to do that the fuzz didn't. He took an attitude and reached for his bread.

As the green was disappearing in the folds of his double-breasted tent, a hard knot formed in my hollow stomach. "How much was there?" I asked sadly.

Fatty had turned to leave. "Twenty-five hundred dollars."

The buxom number hummed a melody in my head and made me think of Southern belles instead of Southern bigots, golden-brown tobacco fields instead of rotten cotton, sprawling green lawns instead of forty rocky acres and a mule. For that kind of money I would've shot my way into Jim Crow's bathroom.

"It's a deal."

Fatty produced the bundle of green joy, along with a thick brown envelope, and tossed them on my desk. "The people I want investigated are very wealthy, very powerful and very dangerous," he warned. "There'll be another twenty-five hundred waiting in the Mecklenberg County Sheriff's office, *if* you bring in the murderer."

I waited for Fatty to tell me more, but that was it and I assumed the brown envelope contained whatever data I would need. I nodded and without further ado he miraculously manipulated his extensive ass out.

The first thing I did was treat myself to a giant milkshake and a huge MacDonald hamburger. While I chomped down I went over the contents of the envelope. T. C. Wharton, sixth in a long line of Southern industrialists, was dead at the age of sixty-two. The causes of his demise were gunshot wounds, two in the upper chest, one in the jaw and another at the base of the skull, delivered by a person or persons unknown. Except for an ancient butler, all of the suspects were members of the Wharton family. Local police had conducted a cursory investigation, but afraid to delve too deep or step on any toes they had come up with a blank. The last item in the envelope really tickled the old innards. It was a document making me an official Mecklenberg County detective. My name had already been typed in, so Fatty must have known all along I was hungry enough to accept any assignment. Twelve hours later I cruised into Whartonville, Virginia, with all flags flying. I could have made it in seven, but once south of Baltimore I didn't push the old Chev past forty.

Whartonville turned out to be just what I expected, a creepy little burg, stuffed into two blocks on one side of the highway. If it hadn't been for the "caution slow" sign, I probably would have breezed right past the whole shebang. The driveway leading to the Wharton estate was longer than the town and by the time I navigated my gasping steed up the elm-shaded lane, she was flapping at the fenders.

There was a fleeting instant when I wondered if I was in the right state because the elegant mansion towering over me and my trembling heap was a brother to the White House. My fears were quickly dispelled as, in answer to softly chiming bells, a fugitive from an Uncle Ben's rice box ushered me through a long vestibile and into a spacious drawing room. Spacious? They could have held the NCAA playoffs there and still had room for a crap game.

They were all waiting when Uncle Ben escorted me in and announced my name. At least I wouldn't have to be tracking anybody across a burning desert or something. Angelie, T.C.'s grey-haired widow, reclined regally in a flower-colored occasional chair near an unlit fireplace. She didn't get up when I walked in. Her dark-haired son, Everett, sprawled at one end of an overstuffed sofa. He didn't acknowledge my presence either. Everett's spouse was the one I couldn't figure. Charlotte Wharton sat on the sofa also, but as far away from Everett as she could get. She was a slutty looking redhead with thick pouting lips and tits ready to bust holes in a black leather shirt. And lastly there was Uncle Ben, somewhere in his late seventies, middle nineties or over the century mark. His bony frame was just that, a frame, and if it hadn't been for the black tails and pants he could have hid behind a table leg. A shock of snow-white hair was his only saving feature.

I didn't see any sense in bullshitting, so I told them why I was there and got right to it. I started with the old lady. "You were by the door?"

The hawk-faced bitch twittered. "Is that what the police told you?"

I knew right then and there that if I planned to accomplish anything, I would first have to shake some of the dust out of the old bag's drawers. I stuck my ugly black face an inch from her beak and fixed her with my pimp sneer. "Lady, we're on different wave lengths, but if you know what's happening you'll tune into my station pretty goddamn quick! You might have these local yokels scared, but not Charles E. Johnson. Now, when I ask a question, I want an answer and not a whole lot of smart mouth! Comprehende?"

Too bad the Academy Awards Committee wasn't on hand because that little Lee Marvin bit would have won an Oscar hands down; but my performance didn't even phase Angelie Wharton. Amused crinkles joined the crow tracks already around her eyes and she looked at me like I was wacked out. Everett was another matter and he jumped up sputtering indignantly. The minute he opened his mouth I knew why Charlotte was at the other end of the sofa.

"Now thee here! You cawn't . . ."

I pulled open my Brooks Brothers jacket, far enough for him to see the walnut butt of "Old Equalizer" and to convince him that I was not the Chattanooga Shoe Shine Boy alone in Dixie.

"You have no right to employ these gestapo methods," he blustered. "You're not the police!" He fluttered his eyelashes and sat down.

"Wrong, Miss Thing," I said, patting my breast pocket. "T.C.'s friends got me a bonafide commission from the county sheriff. You're talking to John Q. System, and don't you forget it."

Angelie snorted through her neb. "How absurd. T.C. had no friends, not even when he was alive."

"He was a despicable brute," Everett put in.

I had been wondering myself just what Fatty's motives were in footing the bill for this private probe. But then, with nearly twenty-five hundred big ones bulging my back pocket and the prospect of twenty-five more, mine was not to question, merely to serve.

To cover my confusion, I pulled out my rent receipt and studied it like it was the secret plans to the X-15. I was bogged down in "crackerland" with a hag, a fag, a tramp, and a relic from *Gone with the Wind,* and I didn't know which way was up. I remembered a phrase once uttered by a noted basketball coach during halftime—"The best defense is offense"—and I started firing questions, using what I had gathed from Fatty's brown envelope as a base.

"After the lights went out and the shots were fired, who turned them back on again?"

"I did," Angelie volunteered, much to my astonishment.

"No one left the room, until after the police arrived?"

Angelie nodded stifly.

"Who called the police?"

Charlotte was in the middle of a tired yawn. "I . . . . . . I . . . "

"Was the phone in T.C.'s room?"

Charlotte giggled. "If nobody left the room, where else could it be?" She stuck her tongue out at me.

Worldly as Charlotte Wharton appeared, I still think she would have blushed at the names I called her under my breath.

"No one saw from which direction the gun flashes came?"

They dummied up on me again: Charlotte jiggled her ass around on the sofa and picked at the hem of a green micro-mini; Angelie stared icily into the fireplace; and Everett's main preoccupation was smoothing down his eyebrows with a spit-moistened finger. I hadn't been paying much attention to Uncle Ben, not really considering him to be a suspect, and I almost fainted when he opened his mouth.

"Sir?"

I swallowed my excitement and forced myself to sound cool. "Yeah?"

"Shouldn't I be about my duties?"

I fought down the urge to shoot the old bastard in the kneecaps and contented myself with a growl. "Just stay where the hell you're at!"

They had me jammed. No question about it; I was up against a blank wall. All four admitted to being in T.C.'s room when the shots were fired, yet no one saw the actual killing or from which direction the shots came. Now, I'd done some night fighting in the Korean fiasco and sometimes all we had to shoot at were gun flashes. So, it was clear that all four were fibbing: three to cover up for the killer and the other one to save his/her ass. About that time an idea crossed my mind and I saw a chance to cut the list of suspects in half.

"You and Twinkle Toes are the only ones with a legitimate claim on T.C.'s big bucks," I said to Angelie.

The old bag was swift and headed me off at the pass. "T.C. was very fond of Charlotte, wasn't he dear? The contents of the will haven't been revealed as yet, but I'm positive he made some provisions for her."

Charlotte made an unlady-like gesture with her middle finger. "I couldn't stand that old frog."

Angelie made her eyes big and gasped in mock surprise. "You certainly could have fooled me," Everett added, putting in his two cents.

Charlotte looked from one to the other and stood up. "How can you say that? We all . . . " A cold glare from Angelie shut her up and she sat down.

Rather than simplify things, the last little byplay only opened up several new avenues. Charlotte could have killed T.C. in the role of jilted mistress, while Angelie, suspecting her husband of a *tete a tete,* was also a prime candidate for the hot seat. No matter how hard I tried, I couldn't picture Everett as the jealous husband though; but the way things had been shaping up I didn't rule out the possibility. The only one who didn't seem to have a beef with T. C. Wharton was Uncle Ben.

"How come you hated T.C.?" I asked Charlotte, not really expecting a sensible answer.

"I'm not answering any more questions," she mumbled.

I figured it was time for some good old fashioned shock therapy, so I grabbed a fistfull of Charlotte's red hair and jerked back hard. I laid a meaty black fist right under her nostrils. "You answer, bitch, or I'll break your motherfucking nose!"

She broke. Goddamned if she didn't! I couldn't have stopped her with a muzzle. "He . . . he . . . made me marry that fag so he could bring me into the house without a scandal! He said if I wanted to stay around I had to . . . He said when he hollered shit . . . for me to roll out like toilet paper! The things he made me do! Ohh . . ." She was a sobbing wreck, but I felt no compassion for her, not after the business she'd given me.

"All he did was use and abuse people," Angelie said dully. "He used his son and he used Charlotte. He used me too, for twenty-six years, and then threw me aside like a dirty handkerchief. He deserved to die."

I wasn't listening, really, because another idea was rooting around in my head. I hadn't pinned the tail on the donkey yet, but indications were that Charlotte was the murderess. If only someone thought her brassy butt was worth saving, Charles Johnson & Associates would have arrived. Angelie's perception was uncanny.

"How much would it cost to send you back where you came from?"

I hesitated, long enough to let her know my doorbell could be rung, then shook my head. "If something like that got out, my business would be ruined."

"Who hired you anyway?"

I shook my head again and laughed. "Sorry, Sis. Obligation to my client and all that jazz." There was no doubt in my mind that if the old lady found out who was paying for this little inquisition, she'd buy Fatty a bed next to some tree roots before morning.

Angelie's smile was a picture of warmth. "Why don't we discuss it further over a drink?"

I felt big. "Scotch and soda." Angelie nodded and Uncle Ben shimmied his way across the gymn to a half-moon-shaped bar.

I moved to the fireplace and leaned my shoulder against the mantle piece. If I worked it right, I was at the end of the rainbow. All I had to do was wait for the pot to fill. When it did, Fatty was one "sold out" piece of blubber. I thought Joe Mannix was full of shit anyway.

Angelie looked me up and down and while she was doing it, her smile changed into a frown. Before I knew it, she was glowering down the bridge of her nose at me. "On second thought," she said, after a few minutes more of deliberation, "the Whartons are famed for making only wise investments. My beloved husband would turn over in his grave if we gave any of his money to a fool."

I didn't know where the bitch got her heart from all of a sudden, since I held the aces. Too late I realized we weren't playing poker.

"I killed Mr. Wharton!"

Talk about shock—Uncle Ben was moving toward me with a .32 revolver in his quivering fist. I clawed at "Old Equalizer" instinctively, but before I could pop the button off my suitjacket, a slug smacked into my navel. Hurting like hell, I watched Angelie take the gun from Uncle Ben. With cold-eyed precision she shot me in the exact spot, making the fire burning my guts out twice at hot. Everett was next and he looked more masculine than Charles Atlas when the silver pistol filled his hand. Instead of shooting me in the stomach, where it already hurt, the bad aim motherfucker shot me in the shoulder. Charlotte ended the "nigger shoot" like Annie Oakley. She bent over, giving me a dying view of her heart covered panties, and aimed upside down between her legs. What marksmanship! That bullet went right through my godamn forehead.

With the desperation of a hard to kill nigger, I clung to the fireplace, cursing myself for my greed. I wanted to live, but the cold blanket of death had decided to tuck me in for good and beckoned me to dream land, right there on the floor of Madison Square Garden. About a second before my black ass touched bottom, it dawned on me—I had just solved my first case. . . .

ALBERT DICKENS
#44714

Dick is a long timer out of Newark, New Jersey, with 7 years in on a 51 year max. Though he aims no poison spears at society, he does feel that ignorance is the real criminal. Of it he says, "too bad someone can't capture it and convert it into a tangible. With ignorance locked in a box, most of the world's troubles would be solved." He is presently enrolled in the college program here at the prison and is hot on the trail of an Associate Arts degree.

ARMAGEDDON

by

Albert Dickens

BROTHER MINISTER ALI MOVED THROUGH THE
war-torn penitentiary, his brown eyes burning with a fierce
fire at the sights of wanton destruction he saw. Although
he himself had lived by violence for many years, he disliked
the senselessness of conflicts such as this, of men who attacked one another for the vaguest of reasons, who fought
without any chance of victory. In his own way, Ali was an
idealist, and he resented the sights of strife which this war
brought. But, he had been taught to stay remote, to observe
from a distance, to keep above the morass of sentiment and
emotion in which these men struggled.

For centuries the Mean Machine had ruled these con-
fines, mostly men without conscience or moral creed, un-
heedful of reasons for their malicious acts. Ali was not like

them, though he was capable of cruelty and malovence. Yet, he could love and hate more violently than even his keepers. It was these strong passions that had caused him to break with society, that had brought him east to have vengeance on a man who had violated his sister. Love and hate; they had brought him to this city of steel and bricks for the remainder of his life. Love and hate; they welled in him now, as a bitter smoke that stung his throat. Love and hate; they had sent him in search of two of his brothers, who had become separated from the others. He could not find them.

His journey took him through an alleyway, between two rows of buildings, gutted by fire, their seared rafters casting cold silhouettes against a bleak sky. Near the print shop, half structure and half hole in the earth, a cawing voice called out his name.

"Brother Minister Ali."

Ali turned his somber brown face in the direction of the voice. A ragged figure in overalls materialized from the wrecked shadows and beckoned him closer.

"How do you know my name?" Ali asked.

"Who could not recognize that proud face," the old man replied.

"I have a feeling there is more to this than chance recognition," Ali said warily. "Who are you and what do you want of me?"

"I am an harmless old stool pigeon," the wretch said. "Would'st thou guest with me a while?"

Ali shook his head and the old man made a mock bow. "So, the mighty minister disdains to grace me with a moment. Does he not even wonder why I stopped him?"

"That is an interesting question," Ali said thoughtfully.
"Why?"

The cur moved closer. "Troopers arrived a few hours
ago from the capitol. They've swept through the cell blocks
and the mess hall. I was in the mess hall and when I saw
the Mean Machine hordes about to engulf me, I fell on my
knees and begged to be spared.

"And what would ye do in return?" asked a Mean Machine officer.

"Anything," I quoth.

"Then bear this message to the Muslim known as Ali,"
the officer said. "Tell him to keep his brothers out of it.
Tell him that if he plays his role well, there will be con-
sideration for him at the next parole board meeting."

"So, I fixed the message in my mind and now give it to
thee."

"What else did you give for this immunity?" Ali asked.

"Why, my soul, of course," the wretch said smiling.

"You nor your soul are of any value," Ali said. "Why
did you not fall like a man?"

"I wish to live," the cur said simply. "But let me not
keep you, Brother Minister, for you must have weightier
matters on your mind." The old man gave another mock
bow and slunk back into the shadows.

Ali goaded himself into a trot. At a sudden gust of
rain from nowhere, he turned up the collar of his khaki
jacket. Another few feet and he was through a gate and
into the big yard. His brothers were where he had left them,
all grouped together in the weight-lifters corner. The bar-
bell box had been broken open and many had armed them-

selves. Ali was their leader by choice, and with the blessings of Elijah.

Captain Kareem stepped forward, his dreary segregation garb contrasting sharply with the khaki's the others wore. He had been freed from his cell during the initial outburst, after several prisoners had stormed the lock-up unit. He was a lifer, with ten years in, and though miniature in a physical sense he demanded respect from all men and got it.

"Are the rumors true?" Captain Kareem asked.

Ali was puzzled. "What rumors?"

"That you would not aid the other prisoners in the upcoming battle."

Ali smiled thinly. "The decision is not mine. Elijah says that we are not to participate in any violence, unless directly assaulted."

"And what does Allah say?" one young brother shouted insolently.

Brother Minister Ali stared hard at the young man for a long time, biting back a reprimand, realizing that everyone was weary, that tempers were short. There was a good cause for this, since the Muslims had been trapped in the middle of this ridiculous rebellion for nearly a week. Ali himself had been caught and confined in his own cell block for three days, joining up with his brothers only after some prisoners had smashed a hole through one of the walls.

"Elijah, God, Allah," Ali said in an even voice. "They are one and the same."

"What of the attacks on Lieutenant Mutakabbir and Brother Akbar?" Kareem asked.

Ali did not know about this. "What attacks?"

Brother Lieutenant Mutakabbir stepped forward, his proud dark face puffed and disfigured, his left arm twisted uselessly at his side. "Early this morning the forces of the Mean Machine stormed our block," he said through torn and blood-scabbed lips. "Brother Akbar and I thought it would be wise if we sat together in his cell. The troopers spared no one, innocent or guilty, participant or non-participant. When they started on Brother Akbar I intervened. They sprayed me with mace and beat me senseless."

Lieutenant Mutakabbir and Brother Akbar had been the objects of Ali's search. No wonder he could not find them. They had made their way by another route. "Why doesn't Brother Akbar speak for himself?"

"He isn't here," Lieutenant Mutakabbir replied. "When I regained consciousness, Brother Akbar was not in the cell with me. My thought is that they killed him and carried away his body."

"Then the way is clear," Ali said softly, his pain and concern evident on his troubled brown face. He took a deep breath and let it out slowly. "Arm yourselves with what you can find. We must defend ourselves, though I dislike being aligned with Caucasians and Nazis."

With the Muslims straggling behind him, scarcely a hundred, but hardened by a strict diet and rigid exercise, Ali made his way across the yard to a canvas-covered backstop that served as a pavilion for the leaders of the rebellion. Paglioni, a self-styled Nazi, nodded cautiously as Ali moved under the tarp. There had always been a certain emnity between the two, since the race riots of '63 and '64, but both realized that, for the present at least, the common enemy was the Mean Machine. Ali turned immediately to the matter of the forthcoming battle.

"What are our chances of success?"

"There is no question of victory," Paglioni answered. "The resources of the Mean Machine are without end. However, their mace and tear gas will be ineffective, as long as the rain holds out. They have men on the walls also, but their orders are not to shoot, unless an attempt is made to escape."

"Then let us lose like men," Ali said gravely, and moved out into the rain. He could have remained under the canvas, among the captains of the convict army, but he felt that his place was with his brothers. Kareem stepped to his side and placed a home-made knife into his hand.

Now, in the grey dusk, the army of the Mean Machine poured unopposed through the gate and spread out across the yard, a tide of swarthy men in blue uniforms, wearing gold badges and white helmets, carrying shields and long night sticks. Dogs prowled among them, showing sharp fangs that could rip a man's throat out.

Paglioni shouted a command and the prisoners moved out to meet the minions of the Mean Machine. Represented in the convict army were Caucasians, Chicanos, Black Panthers, even a few Orientals. In the center of the phalanx rushed the Muslims.

"Fight in the name of Allah!" Ali cried above the hissing rain.

Beside Ali moved Kareem, his damp segregation shirt loose on his small frame. He echoed Ali's cry with one of his own. "Do not falter! Allah will send help when we least expect it!"

89

The two forces crashed and Ali found himself face to face with a Mean Machine officer. The snarling autocrat's features wrinkled into an evil grin. "We thought you would be here, nigger, and we have a special fate planned for you!"

"Too many swine know my destiny better than I," Ali retorted, "but if I deal with you here, there will be one less to manipulate it."

Ali struck at the blue chest, but his blade glanced off the heavy mesh shield the Mean Machine officer held before him. As he lunged in again, a heavy club fell on the side of his head and he crumpled to his knees, blood gushing from a gash six inches long. Through a haze he saw the officer preparing to smash him again and knew that if the blow landed he would never rise again. It was then that the little captain jumped between them, a knife in each hand, like a giant in his confidence. The Mean Machine officer moved away.

"If you live, Ali," he called back, "I will seek you out."

Kareem kept a space cleared, until Ali had cleared the fog from his spinning head and moved back into the fray. The minister cut an enemy trooper, then another, slashed now a Shepherd dog that lashed at him with bared teeth. Blood ran down his face, his shoulder throbbed, his arm ached, but he lifted the shiv again and again. A loud groan from the other prisoners made him look up and he saw the Nazi, surrounded on all sides by Mean Machine troopers. The huge blond giant fought magnificently and on several occasions it seemed as if he might break free, but the outcome was inevitable and he soon disappeared under a swarm of white helmets and walnut colored clubs.

90

It was the beginning of the end and the convict army began falling back in ragged groups. The Muslims maintained their composure and retreated in a body, a step at a time. As they neared the back wall, fresh Mean Machine troops came over the top, dropping on them from above. Ali was at despair's bottom when he felt the tug of Kareem's hand on his arm.

"The Mean Machine rules here!" the little captain said. "Let us look to our own predicament!" He cupped his hands around his mouth and yelled. "Everybody away from the walls!"

For the life of him Ali could not comprehend what Kareem was about. They were hemmed in on all sides by Mean Machine troops and high stone walls. He was still trying to figure it out when the grey clerestory suddenly erupted into a million fragments. When the smoke cleared there was a breech fifty feet wide. Kareem's plan became explicitly clear. "Allah will send help when we least expect it!" he had cried, just before the battle. And indeed He had.

Scarcely thinking, Ali led his brothers through the gap. A few stragglers found themselves facing opposition, as the Mean Machine recovered quickly and blocked the avenue to freedom. Among those still trying to clear the breech was Captain Kareem, and it was here that a bullet spun him around in a circle. The atomite refused to go down though, fought his way out of the confusion and caught up with Ali, who had scattered the other brothers, feeling that separation increased everyone's chances of getting away. They moved toward distant hills. Ali was prepared to slow down, to carry his brother if necessary, but Kareem clasped a hand to his abdomen and matched him step for step.

They were still moving briskly when night descended. The rain had stopped and the moon hung brightly in a starlit sky. Ali would have preferred the storm, for there was better security in the darkness, but if they could reach the hills before daybreak . . .

Two hours later Kareem sagged to his knees. Ali bent to lift him up, but the little captain shook him off.

"You must leave me."

Ali knew that Kareem's death was just a matter of time, but he sat down alongside of his brother. He made an attempt at joviality. "Desert my little iron captain? No way!"

"You must go," Kareem groaned painfully, clutching at his stomach. "Many of us will be recaptured, but the Brother Minister Ali Muhammad must not be caught. You have a responsibility."

Ali shook his head, wishing that the blood seeping through the tiny tan fingers was his own. "While you live and breathe, so will I sit here with you. Be it the will of Allah."

Kareem reached feebly into his waistband and brought out a crude knife, similiar to the one he had given Ali back in the prison yard. Before Ali knew his intention, he had plunged the rusty iron into his own breast. "Peace . . . Peace . . . ," he managed to murmur, and tumbled into a limp heap beneath the universe.

It was some time before Ali could think coherently again, some time before the tears stopped watering his tormented face, some time before he realized that the wound in his head had broken open and that blood had joined the tears. When he finally looked up it was as if the world had taken on a new shape and he found that he stood on a rocky plain at the foot of a huge mountain.

He took off his jacket and covered the little captain with it. "Peace, Kareem," he whispered. "Allah has truly blessed you." He straightened up, took a deep breath, and started into the hills.

LET THERE BE LIGHT

by

Albert Dickens

THE FIRST THING PAUL HAYDEN SAW WHEN HE opened his eyes was the head of the thing. The slitted eyes were red with fire and its teeth were fangs, protruding over thick purple lips. There were high bushy brows, patches of shiny skin under the cheekbones and a wide stubby nose with two flaring pink nostrils. The rest of the mammoth hulk was covered with a thick mat of blue fur, but for the fingers, which ended in green pick-like claws.

Paul stared in awe through the faceplate of his helmet. What sort of monster could stand the furnace-like elements of Venus, could breathe the suffocating air and live? Would the thing attack him? Did its eating diet include flesh? How long would he live if one of those needle-sharp claws ripped through his insulated suit? Outside, the lightning flashed, spraying the interior of the cave with scintillating nuances.

The roar of the fire storm and brilliant multi-colored flashes only made the creature's dreadfulness all the more frightening. The astronaut moved, unconsciously, and his air tanks grated noisily against the wall of the cave. The brute roared, twisted and rose, saliva dribbling from the corners of its fanged mouth. As the beast lumbered toward him, bellowing loudly and pounding its huge chest, Paul scrambled backwards, searching desperately about for an avenue of escape. Near the back he tripped over a mound of rocks and fell headlong.

The first manned landing on Venus had been carried out in much the same manner as the Apollo series on the Moon. Since the gravitational pull of Venus more than tripled that of Luna, it was simply a matter of providing stronger retro-rockets for the landing module. Lieutenant Hayden had been assigned to pilot the landing craft, *Aphrodite,* while Major Norris Winfield commanded the mother ship in an orbit forty miles above the surface of Venus. As had been expected, due to the ion-charged atmosphere and the intense heat which ranged from 104 degrees Fahrenheit to 539 degrees, radio contact was impossible.

For the same two reasons, plus the absence of nitrogen, the possibility of intelligent life forms had been ruled out. Paul's instructions were to land, collect rock and soil samples, and take off again. At no time was he to wander more than a few feet from the *Aphrodite*. But man's curiosity is an overpowering thing and when he saw movement on the crest of a low hill he went to investigate.

A hundred yards from the landing module a calm rainbow-colored sky erupted suddenly into lances of blue and red flames. He was driven down and into unconsciousness. When he opened his eyes he was in the cave, and the thing was there.

The brute knelt over Paul, taloned hands thrust high in the air as if paying homage to some great being before the feast. Warm tears of appeal joined the perspiration on the young astronaut's cheeks and he dug his faceplate deeper into the dusty floor of the cave. He steeled himself for the first ripping slash of the green claws, but the beast touched his shivering form tenderly. The incarnadine eyes still glowed with fury, but they had also acquired an assuasiveness and reflected memories of a nearly forgotten past. A moment later the thing rose silently and plodded out of the cave. Scarlet blue flames pelted its matted hide, but the storm hardly annoyed the beast and it waved a lazy arm and disappeared.

On legs turned to rubber, Paul wobbled to the mouth of the cave, where billowy clouds of vermillion and periwinkle floated aimlessly about in a sky of depthless black, flaring intermittenly into bolts of irridescent fire. At another time, in another situation, he would have taken time to marvel at the display of giant fireworks. He would have attempted to solve some of the mystery surrounding the creature who had saved his life, but at the moment it was all he could do to keep from racing in the direction of the *Aphrodite,* squatting a few hundred feet away like a dark insect on the scorched landscape. Common sense prevailed though. It would be suicide to try it before the storm abated.

Paul moved to the rear of the cave and the mound of rocks he had tripped over earlier. The small heap seemed to represent a sort of altar and a closer study revealed a square manufactured object jutting out from under the pile. He removed several rocks carefully and uncovered a book, cloth bound and centuries old. He picked it up gingerly, but the cover and several pages crumbled in his gloved hands. For the pages that remained intact, time had acted as erasure. It was near the back that he finally found a trace of legible print. He leaned closer and from the light supplied by the periodic flashes of the storm, he began to read. And as he read, he began to tremble. . . .

> *But the day of the Lord will come*
> *As a thief in the night*
> *In the which the heavens shall pass away*
> *With a great noise*
> *And the elements shall melt*
> *With fervent heat*
> *The earth also*
> *And the works that are therein*
> *Shall be burned up.*

JOHN J. JONES
#36514

J. J. comes from Newark, New Jersey, walking straight under a 65-year-load. His thing is singing and he can be heard early in the morning, late at night or just about any time of the day doing just that. Oddly, enough, in this world abundant with disgruntled people, nobody ever complains. Why should they when the sound they hear is a cross between Johnny Mathis and Billy Eckstine? It makes one wonder just how far J. J. could have gone in the music world, had the proper opportunities been available to him.

THE PASSING OF BIG JOE

by

John J. Jones

EVERYONE CALLED HIM BIG JOE, EXCEPT FOR my mother and I. It never occurred to me that he would die, no more than I could think of the sun falling out of the sky. But he was dead, and he just lay there, clothed in a suit made out of his favorite shade of blue. He didn't seem dead though and his smoothly shaven face appeared so alive that I wouldn't have been surprised if he climbed out of that coffin, faked a laughing swipe at my head, wrapped his big arms around my mother and me and took us home.

He was stronger than any man alive, yet despite his ponderous size, he was gentler than a baby with those he loved. On the other hand, he demanded respect, and those who didn't give him his due soon found out that Big Joe

100

wasn't a man to be toyed with. When aroused, my father was a veritable tiger.

In my earlier years, it used to puzzle me no end, when relatives would visit my mother and talk about him disparagingly. Perhaps they thought I was too young to understand what they were saying, and they were right, because in later years I still couldn't figure out why Big Joe was the source of so much envy. Physically, he was more capable than any of them and the same was true of his financial abilities, yet he never hesitated when a favor was needed, even if it meant his last dime. It was some time before I fully realized the undercurrent of hostility my father's kin felt for him, though I never could understand their reasoning. Perhaps it was his natural generosity that caused the resentment, or perhaps they realized their own inadequacies in the competence he emanated.

As I sat in the funeral parlor, handcuffed between two burly black prison guards, I watched the members of the Jones clan file past Big Joe's coffin. Uncle Ridgeway led the line, his face fixed rigidly in the appropriate pose of grief. Behind him came Uncle Sterling, his wrinkled features reflecting fear and guilt, his mustard-colored eyes darting to and from Big Joe's motionless form. No one would have guessed that these two had initiated a plot to steal Big Joe's leather business, while he lay helpless in a hospital bed.

All I could do was sit there, too hurt to cry, too numb to speak. The sobs of the truly grieved filled the death-permeated atmosphere, making the pseudo-mourners appear shallow by contrast. It was with a sigh of relief that I felt one of the prison guards tapping me on the shoulder, indicating it was time to go.

Outside, my escorts had to make a path through a crowd of people who had come to pay their last respects to Big Joe. Heads turned as I passed by. Just before I stooped to enter the back seat of the prison station wagon, I heard a man's voice.

"Wasn't dat Big Joe's boy?"

"Sho nuff. It's just like Big Joe spit the boy out."

"Mebbee the old son ain't daid afta all."

After the door with no handles closed me in and the station wagon had moved out into a stream of traffic, I let it all go, no longer able to stop the tears from washing my face. I wondered if the two men knew what they were talking about, if they even knew Big Joe or that my name was John.

Big Joe was dead. A blind man could see that.

JAMES (55X) WASHINGTON
#44501

James' main bag is poetry, but this versatile individual took a break from his metaphors and similes and contributed "It Only Happens Once." Just recently he received a time cut, reducing a 51-year sentence to 30 years. It couldn't have happened to a nicer guy.

IT ONLY HAPPENS ONCE

by

James (55X) Washington

HIS SISTER'S VOICE ASSAULTED HIM FROM THE
yard and he winced, a prisoner of words that analyzed, un-
justly tried to explain him. Florence sat on the porch with
Ruth Hopkins, an old bag out from town.

"He's always been that way, never accepting an end to
anything. I don't understand him. He was never nice to her,
never smiled, never talked, just grunts and nods. The only
time he laughed was after he had swallowed a gallon of
that home-made corn liquor."

He rolled over on the hay pile. Part of him believed
she knew he was in the barn listening. She had no idea
where he was, really, nor what was on his mind either. He
had been stunned when Laney died and walked through
the fields for hours. The next day he got angry about nothing and cried bitterly. Perhaps it was because he had let

104

Laney down by not crying before.

Florence coughed, a hacking rattle. She was tough as nails, eighty-one and still in everybody else's business. He wished she would go home and take Ruth with her. They yakked like a pair of old hens, not like Laney, who knew when to talk and when to keep her mouth shut.

"Ohh . . . , he's off somewhere. Hasn't done a bit of work since it happened, not that he done much when she was here. Don't know why he's grieving so. He was always complaining about everything she did, and he never gave her anything—nothing to show he appreciated having her around."

He looked at his clothes, the bibbed coveralls stained with dirt and grease, the tattered grey shirt with both elbows worn out, the scarred tips of his brogans. Never gave her anything? Never had any damn thing to give! Did good just to eat.

"He must have cared some Flo." Ruth sounded like a grouchy bull frog. She looked like one, too. Wasn't any wonder old Fred Hopkins' eyes went bad on him. "They stayed together almost fifty-three years. Some people just keep their feelings hid."

He wished Ruth would shut her trap, especially since she didn't know what she was cackling about. It wasn't *almost* fifty-three years! It *was* fifty-three years and seven months. Just thinking about it made him feel old, older than his seventy-four years, and useless. He tried to force part of himself away, so that it wouldn't hurt so much, so he wouldn't be totally involved. Nearly forgotten memories slipped past the erected barriers anyway.

When he was young he used to sit by the river and talk to the rolling water. It was his favorite place because the rushing quicksilver only listened, never nagged, never sassed him back.

"Why are you so sad?"

Eyes as clear as eyes could get, hair like a winter night, skin, brown and flawless. He never saw her before. Later, he found out her pa sharecropped the Thompson place on the other side of the river. She was with him from that day on . . . until now. . . .

He caught himself. Emotion was a hostile thing, crouching, waiting to destroy him. Sweat, from the mid-August heat ran down the bridge of his nose and into his eyes, but he didn't rub it away. He wasn't going to let things like that bother him anymore. Laney didn't, always looking at the bright side—the brilliance of a summer sun, not the sweltering heat, the itching, the flies; the pureness of a first snow, not the icy cold, the slush, the road-blocking drifts. She even had something good to say about dying: "It only happens once."

The memories grew stronger and when the crouched thing sprang, he stopped fighting and the tears came, hot, salty, streaking his prune-colored, white-whiskered cheeks. He crawled to a back window and looked out at the untended cornfield standing like red gold, the wine-washed sun dying in a dull-blue horizon, the uncomplaining tips of the giant firs by the river.

Laney came back then, but in a different way, and the torment began to fade. Soon it was gone entirely and a wild exuberance engulfed him. He dove headfirst back into the haypile and lay there for a moment, enjoying a blissful weightlessness. Then he probed around near the bottom of the brown-green grass, until his hand curled around the neck of his specially-brewed jug of white lightning.

The first gulp brought a sharp gasp, a hot shiver, an idiotic giggle. He staggered up. Another snort spun him into the loose hinged barn door and out into the yard. He swayed sideways and plopped down on the seat of his overalls.

The two women glanced up quickly and he grinned stupidly at them, a gaping hole surrounded by purple gums. Florence smiled in spite of herself. After she fixed him something to eat she could go home. The old fool was back to normal.

PAUL M. FITZSIMMONS
#36769

Fitz, probably the best writer in the prison system, comes from Lyndonville, Vermont. A graduate of the Famous Writers School, he is trying to outlast a life bid so that he can put his talent to work on the outside. Two years ago, after finding it nearly impossible to break into the major markets from behind the walls, he became disgusted with the whole business and packed his manuscripts under his bed. They were gathering dust when we told him we were trying to put together a collection of stories written by convicts. "The Napkin Ring" and "The Green Door" are only two of many beautiful pieces written by this man.

THE NAPKIN RING

by

Paul M. Fitzsimmons

IN PLACE OF THE USUAL CARILLON BELLS SIG-
naling the hour of lauds, the harsh thump of hobnailed
boots jarred Sister Domenica awake. She slipped from her
plain plank bed and dressed quickly in the drab grey robes
of a novitiate. Before joining a stream of nuns headed for
the refectory, she snatched a silver napkin ring from beneath a loose stone in the floor and dropped it into her only
pocket.

When the women were all assembled an imposing army
officer stepped to a wide oak lectern at the head of the
room. "Reverend Sisters, I am Colonel Aguirre, of the
nationalist Army of Spain." The tone of his voice and the
expression on his broad face bespoke of urgency. "The Republicans are advancing on Numantia Sona and the convent
stands directly in their path. For this reason it must be

abandoned." As if to add emphasis to his words, a battery of artillery opened up in the north. He smiled faintly and stalked from the room.

Rustling robes sounded like a breeze stirring a pile of dried leaves. Mother Superior told them that the novitiates would have to return to their homes, while the other sisters, those who had taken their vows and sworn their lives to God, would move in a body to the convent at Velencia. The old woman prayed with the novitiates as a group, then individually, giving money and advice to each.

"This is best for you, Luz," Mother Superior said fondly when it was Sister Domenica's turn to say *adieu*. Sister Domenica giggled nervously, unable to believe the fortunate turn of events. She was going home! She was going to Aranda! She would be Luz Escudera Y Cortez again. "Have you not wondered why," the Superior went on, "after four years your vows were never taken? You were not meant for this life." The old woman held up a finger reproachfully. "But that doesn't mean you should love Him less." She gently removed Luz's coif and wimple, loosing, a swirl of waist-length black hair. "Find other apparel. There is something about the virginity of women that attracts men far more than if she were otherwise." The old woman sighed. "At least I won't have to turn my head when you go to your hiding place in the floor of your cell. Begone . . . before I cry. . . .

So it was that Luz Escudera Y Cortez returned to the turbulent world of war-torn Spain in the summer of 1936. The dusty half kilometer between Numantia Sona and the convent snaked ahead of her like a curling carpet of gold.

The sky seemed a shade bluer and even the birds in the road lining eucalyptus trees sounded more cheerful.

Unchanged, since the days of Moorish conquest, Numantia Sona squatted on the dry plain of Castile. It was a town of no consequence, except during olive season, when it overflowed with workers and greedy government tax collectors. Dried brick houses and buildings bent over Luz tiredly, weary from standing for ages over the cobblestone streets. She saw few soldiers and the idea of being raped or murdered seemed farfetched. But, she was not an ignorant girl and realized that Mother Superior spoke with a certain wisdom. So, she hurried through the streets, peering fruitlessly into each shop window, searching for something that a sixteen-year-old girl could wear. As the hours slipped by she began to grow frantic.

"What is it you seek, little one?"

A heavy, mustachioed woman stood in the doorway of a clothing shop. Behind her ranged an abundance of dresses, but their gaudy colors and frills were indicative of the *gitana* women.

"Please help me! I must not be caught by the Republican dogs in these robes!"

Flesh-rippling laughter shook the coarse woman. "They are not dogs, wee one, just men." She studied Luz carefully and sighed. "I will never understand why the prettiest ones always hide themselves away in convents."

Reluctantly, Luz strolled past the woman toward a rack of flaunty, colored dresses. With a sinking heart she picked out the least garish and removed her robes, until nothing but bloomers and a camisole covered her trim figure. The swish of black hair splayed out over ivory shoulders and framed the upper curves of her budding young breasts. She caught sight of an old, dappled pier glass mirror nearby and looked at herself for the first time in four years. Fascinated, she smiled at her reflection, showing small white teeth in the delicacy of a fine-boned face. The fat woman clucked approvingly.

"If I possessed such loveliness, I would go naked in the streets."

Luz blushed crimson. She slipped quickly into the dress and took a last despairing look at herself in the mirror. A deep cut in the neck of the dress revealed far more than was decent, as did a wide split up the front. Orange and red frills only made the dress more suggestive, but she was in no position to be choosy. She took a handkerchief from her folded robes and proffered a little hoard of money to the plump proprietress. The woman shrugged, but took it.

"The Republicans will steal it anyway."

Luz tucked the napkin ring between cradling young breasts and stepped into the afternoon sun. She followed the serpentine twisting cobbles out of Numantia Sona, to a road that led to the Rio Duero, one hundred kilometers distant. Compared to her staid black stockings and shoes, the dress was an incongruity and at each step the skirt split wide, revealing to the crotch her underthings. She saw few men and these were mostly *viejo's,* men who were too old to fight. Even they whistled appreciatively and thought of years gone by.

"Aiee!" one *viejo* cried. "A night with that one and I would halt the Republican advance by myself."

"Old *cabron,*" another joshed, "a night with her would see you in the grave by sunrise."

113

This was a new experience for Luz and the crude remarks disturbed her. She had always thought of her body as simply a dwelling place for a soul that belonged to God. Now, even old men talked of it openly. Self consciously, she tried to conceal the jut of her breasts by pressing in her arms at the sides. This only made them more prominent and in the end she gave up in frustration.

Luz followed the ribbon of dirt toward home, always in the direction of the Pyrenees, their snow-covered tips bunched together like servings of grey pudding with whipped cream on top. People traveling both ways clogged the rutted highway. From time to time she touched the napkin ring between her breasts, tracing with her fingers the time-worn smoothness between ornate rows of intricately hammered roses. It belonged to Illinea. Luz had snatched it from a table as Jaime was harnessing the burro for the long trip to the convent. Every morning for four years she had cupped it in her tiny hands and kissed the proudly protruding initials, "I E Y C," as if love poured into the cold metal would somehow be conveyed to Illinea and soften her heart. No longer would she have to conceal it, like a pirate hoarding his booty. She was going home.

Night descended, like a plum growing rapidly riper. The long muscles of her legs began to ache and when she spotted the twinkling glow of a roadside fire she hurried to it. A wizened little man with a shock of startling white hair made room for her. She smiled her gratitude and sat on the ground in front of the warm blaze.

"Where are you headed, little one?"

"Across the Rio Duero to Aranda."

"What are you called?"

"Luz Esudera Y Cortez."

The old man squinted thoughtfully. "From Aranda, you say . . . ? Is your father Jaime, the *alcade?*"

"Do you know him? Have you seen him?" Luz spoke quickly and anxiously. "Is he well? Does he . . ."

"Slowly, pigeon," the old man said, stopping her rapid flow of questions. "I know Jaime well and also your mother Illinea. But I haven't been to Aranda in some time." He turned to a pack at his side. "You look hungry. We will eat and talk more of Aranda." He handed Luz a square of cheese and some rolls.

She spent a pleasurable night, talking with the old man, the others around the fire, Aranda, her family, Spain. With the coming of the sun the easy comradeship dissipated and people hurried away from the smouldering coals, once again strangers, each going a singular way.

Luz moved constantly toward the Pyrenees, whose majestic peaks seemed to be straining for heaven—step after weary step, kilometer after kilometer, all blending together into boring segments of purple and yellow. On the fourth day the terrain began to change noticably. Sheep and cows grazed on steep green inclines and in the afternoon she reached the Rio Duero.

At a pool formed by a bend in the river she sank beneath a gnarled alder to a mattress of fallen leaves. After a time she waded to the center of the icy-green pool and sat down, letting the cool water ease the pain of tired muscles. Several women chattered furiously nearby and laundered clothes with fine bottom sand. For the most part they ignored her, but one woman's curiosity eventually got the best of her.

115

"Where do you come from?"

"From the convent," Luz said languidly," near Numantia Sona."

The woman burst into guffaws of laughter. She shouted to a crony, who pounded trousers on a rock. *"Oye,* Tanya, from Numantia Sona in that dress!"

"I heard! From the convent also! A nun who flees from God!"

She was the center of attraction now and the old women were merciless. They badgered her endlessly, admonished her for abandoning God in a time of peril—and in the clothes of a whore.

Luz stood up, the wet dress clinging to her like a glove. "What do you know of God?" she shouted scornfully. "What do you know of me?"

With the grace of a fawn she walked from the pool. She was ashamed of her breasts now, her hips, her legs, her beauty, yet knew that she shouldn't be. Hadn't He made her pretty? Before she was out of ear range the craggly wash women were talking of other things.

The same as when liege lords lived in their crumbling grey castles, Aranda clung to the side of the mountain. Tick-tocks of anticipation surged through Luz as she scampered across a slanting green meadow, down the last hillside. Her childhood nature returned and blotted out all memories of the ugly experiences along the road. When she thought of Illinea she experienced a momentary pang of apprehension. But the singing in her heart soon took over again and she ran even faster.

On the outskirts of Aranda she slowed to a walk, touching this thing and that, almost weeping at the renewed acquaintance. To the right was her street, less dusty than the others, and at the very end stood her house, its plainness broken by a white fence and the framing hues of a flower garden. She spread her arms wide and stumbled the last few steps breathlessly.

Illinea sat with her wide back to the door, shelling peas into a pan. Several friends helped her and it was one of these who first spied Luz, her cheek pressed against the sunbaked doorframe.

"Illinea, I think it is your daughter!"

Illinea jumped up, spilling peas and pans to the floor. "Aiee! What are you doing here?"

Luz was taken aback at the viciousness of her mother's tone. "We were told to come home," she said hesitantly. "The convent had to be abandoned because of the Republican Army and there was not room for us all at Valencia."

"Illinea curled her lips distastefully. "A likely tale."

Luz felt the joy of coming home slipping away. There was no change in Illinea's hardness of heart, not even after four years. "Is father here?" she asked weakly.

"Never mind that!" Illinea snapped, her face set like granite. "Have you been in the convent or whoring in a cafe?"

Unlike the impersonal jibes of the *viejo's* or the scornful remarks of the wash women, Illinea's insinuations pierced Luz through. She hung her head. "Why do you shame me, mother?"

"You shame yourself!" Illinea sneered.

Luz repeated her question of Jaime. It was barely coherent. "Where is father?"

"Dead, three months past." Illinea spoke of her husband without emotion. "Better so, than have him see you in the clothes of a *gitana.*"

The shock of Jaime's death shook Luz to the bone and, though stricken with anguish, the realization that she would have to speak for herself now brought her chin up. "I don't know what petty jealousy prompted you to send me to the convent, but I didn't want to go nor did father want to send me away. We were not strong enough to stand against you." She spoke now with the determination of a woman, but a weary one, who liked not the cruelness of maturity. "Now I am home, wearing what I could find, and you call me *gitana.* I say you lie!"

Luz had not raised her voice, but the import of her words hit Illinea like a slap in the face. To speak in such a manner to one's mother was bad enough, but to the widow of Jaime the *alcade?* Aiee! Illinea battered Luz back from the doorway with her great weight. Outside, she snatched up a piece of adobe and struck her daughter in the stomach with it. The claque of women burst from the house and joined her, pummeling Luz with stones, bits of adobe and clods of dirt.

Luz stood helplessly, head bent, trying hard not to wince as the rocks stung her face and arms. Tears gathered blood from uncountable nicks and cuts, fell off her chin and formed little balls of mud on the ground. Then, with the suddenness of a diving falcon, a large rock struck her on the side of the head and she went down. Her skirt flew up around her waist, exposing the long white bloomers of a chaste young girl. The women froze in horror.

"What whore wears them?" one cried.

With the return of reason, Illinea whimpered and fell to her knees. The others glanced sideways at one another and slunk away. When the glittering napkin ring rolled from its nest between Luz's breasts, Illinea uttered a strangled wail and began sobbing convulsively.

The sparkling napkin ring spun in a wobbly circle, caught up the red rays of the dying Spanish sun and reflected them on Luz's face, where streaks of blood were beginning to congeal. She neither blinked nor moved. A moment later the wine-colored orb ducked guiltly behind the pudding cups and towed the daylight in its wake.

THE GREEN HOUSE

by

Paul M. Fitzsimmons

THE TIER OF CONDEMNED MEN'S CELLS PRE-
sented a nauseating sight, everything done in varying shades
of green. Even the door to the execution chamber at the
end of the hall shone a dark green. A funeral quiet ruled
in the house of death, broken only by an occasional com-
ment about law or the chances of someone getting a reversal
through the courts. The cells, though large, were strictly
functional units; a commode, a cot, a washbasin, a table,
all anchored to the floor with huge machine bolts. Blanket
edges were taped, sheets triple hemmed; there were no
matches, no shoe laces, no belts, nothing that would allow
a man the opportunity to cheat society of its vengenance.

Once before Kevin Riordan had eaten the last meal,
listened as the warden read the document that made his
death a legal thing. Once before he had felt the straps

121

tighten around his ankles, thighs, groin, chest and arms. Once before he had stiffened himself in anticipation of the juice that would singe his flesh. When the phone jingled with his reprieve he almost lost his mind and they had to drag him away from the obscene embrace of the electric chair. Now, tonight, they expected him to go through it again. But, long ago he had discarded the thought of dying in such a manner. This time they would have to carry him.

Darkness fell and with it came an unearthly stillness— the augery of the tragedy to come. Kevin ate the last meal methodically, not really tasting the food, though the inmates in the prison cookhouse always put an extra effort into a man's last meal. He finished picking at the food and set the tray on the floor, then started his exercise.

For two years he had been preparing himself for this day, working daily: push ups, squats, knee bends, toe touches, sit ups. Now, when his last breathing hours could be counted on one hand, he stood awesome in his tremendous physical strength. No, this time he had no intention of going like a lamb to slaughter.

An hour later, when they fitted him up with new clothes and shaved his head, he offered no resistance. Then he was alone again, except for the relentless corridor lights and their cold shadows, slicing down windowless walls, sliding through the steel bars and into his cell. There were other prisoners on death row, but each man was sunk into his own thoughts, knowing that what Kevin faced tonight they would have to face another day. Throats were like sandpaper and the few futile words that were offered stuck and died in cottony mouths. Now, Kevin stared at the clock

across the hall, fascinated by the racing red hand that slashed time from his last moments on earth.

The hollow sound of an outer door opening and bang-
ing shut broke the clock's hold on his eyes and the warden
moved in front of his cell, flanked by the prison chaplain
and six husky club-bearing guards. Though he had been
staring at it for a half hour, Kevin glanced quickly at the
clock again, surprised to see that the remorseless hands had
scissored at five to eleven. As the graying prison administra-
tor began reading the death warrant in a scratchy voice,
Kevin moved to the door. The captain of the execution
squad inserted a key into the iron lock and swung the door
wide. Kevin ignored him and spoke to the warden in a flat
voice.

"I want to ask you something."

The warden nodded, his sallow face reflecting the distaste he felt for this part of his job.

"Do you agree with this sort of thing?" Kevin asked.

The warden looked away. "It's the law," he said eva-
sively.

"The law!" Kevin scoffed. "According to the law, it's
first degree murder to plan another man's death. I didn't
plan anything. I pulled a stick-up. I thought I had to shoot
and I did, but I didn't plan it. What you're doing now is
premeditated murder. I want to know how come there's a
double standard."

The warden spread his hands in an exasperated gesture,
shamed and angered that this last distorted act was always
shouldered on him.

"The Lord giveth and the Lord taketh away," the chaplain mumbled.

Kevin laughed bitterly and looked at the man in black. "Don't give me that, Rev. If there is a Lord He got to be one mean mother jumper! And if this is what He thinks about me, your Roman Collar would blush if I told you what I thought about Him."

The captain shifted his heavy club to his right hand. "All right, Riordan, let's go."

Kevin turned his cold eyes on the paunchy captain. "You're going to have to earn your pay tonight," he said softly.

The words, though spoken calmly, shook them all. The captain moved in first, but the low iron doorframe caught his club and splintered it in two. Without further ado Kevin drove a meaty fist into his mouth. The captain staggered backwards, frightened, half conscious, his mouth dribbling blood, but the press of his subordinates forced him at Kevin again, where another fist broke his nose and sent him slithering to the floor in a pot-bellied heap.

The others surged at Kevin, cursing, jabbing with their clubs, but negotiation of the narrow doorway proved to be a problem and he disposed of the first three in short order, throwing one head-first into the back wall, tumbling another into the commode and sliding the third under his bed. But the end result was inevitable and soon the only noise coming from the cell were grunts of expended energy and the sounds of hard wood thudding on flesh and bones.

The tenacious wheels of justice were soon running smoothly again and it was a broken and bleeding man they dragged into the execution chamber. Tight-lipped, breathing heavily, the guards secured the limp hulk to the chair, cruelly pulling the straps extra tight, jamming on the helmet with the black veil in front and the spiked circuit on top. After the ankle electrodes were attached all was in readiness.

Kevion Riordan completely dominated the crowded room. Brine ran from beneath the veil covering his face, mixing with blood from his wounds, making a gory slime on the pristine whiteness of his new shirt. The attending physician scrutinized the condemned man closely, the lolling head, the lax hands lying limp instead of clutching at the last reality they would ever know. He whispered hurriedly to the warden, who gestured quickly to the executioner, who had been peering impatiently from his curtained alcove of rheostats and death-dealing dials.

A keening hum filled the room, causing Kevin's body to lunge against the restraints. Another hum, another lunge, and the stink of cooking meat, sweat and blood. The sound of a witness vomiting was loud and the rustle of nervous movement was like the wind soughing through the branches of a dead forest.

The physician moved forward, stethoscope at the ready, but he only went through the motions of checking the burnt body for signs of life. Only the doctor knew that kevin had never been aware of the agony of being roasted alive. He stepped back, keeping his face averted, nodding in indication that society's due had been extracted from Kevin Riordan.

EUGENE (SAMAD) WATSON
#40915

Samad is a five-foot, five-inch gem out of Newark, New Jersey, on the tenth year of a life bid. A devout Muslim, he is noted for his honesty, an attribute rare in such a place. He spends most of his time writing poetry and playing handball. He likes progressive jazz, is 30 years old, and thinks of life as one long coffee break between two deaths.

THE DROPOUTS

by

Eugene (Samad) Watson

HE LOOKED AROUND THE GROUNDS OF THE UNI-versity, as though seeing them for the first time. There were many new structures, but this was a place of tradition and the old landmarks were still very much in evidence. He walked past a huge boulder, with a tiny peach tree growing out of the top of it. No one knew how the boulder got there, nor how the tree managed to flourish year after year, without benefit of care or the proper soil conditions. He came to the chapel garden and strolled through it, experiencing the pain of sadness, knowing that this place had forgotten him, had been leading its own varied existence.

On the far side of the garden, tables and decorations had been set up on the grass. Students danced and music floated across the flower tops, and as the orchestra played it seemed a voice far, far above began to cry. He listened more closely and this time found the voice imperious, insisting that he leave and never return. Then suddenly the mood changed and there was boisterous laughter and gay chatter. The warm dusk, the fragrance of the grass and trees, embellished the convivial feeling. He found himself drifting toward the festivities.

Yesterday's students took flowers from the tables and made bouquets for their girls, or strewed the petals in their hair. He did not know the young girl who sat across from him, with small brown eyes and wearing a lavender gown that made her appear childish. She did not dance and he wondered if it was because she was shy, or if she did not know how. Of the girls still seated at the tables, only she had no bouquet, no petals in her hair, no one bending over her in pleasant conversation. She smiled anyway, as if to show that she was a part of it all and as happy as anyone else. Someone dropped a rose carelessly on the chair beside her. She picked it up and stuck it in her hair.

"Hello."

She looked at him, liking his large clear eyes and wide sensitive mouth, which seemed to be ready for both joy and grief. She wondered about his age. It didn't show on his face or in his manner. "Hello."

Her voice did not sound shy and he liked the tone of it, thin, yet somehow solid—flat, yet somehow musical. "I was about to leave, but if I could persuade you to dance with me, perhaps I might stay a while."

She hesitated, about to refuse, then for no apparent reason changed her mind and offered her hand. He stepped around the table and bowed, like a courtier of old, then led her smoothly into the circle of dancers. They danced . . .

and danced . . . and danced . . . , until the slate—grey night began to recede before a shimmering yellow sun.

"I think we should say goodbye now."

He looked at her quickly. "A while longer. . . . Please . . . I'll be leaving soon. . . . I may never return. . . ."

She nodded and they walked toward the university town. As the long rows of buildings drew them on he looked at her from time to time, discomfitted to remember that he had not thought her pretty. In front of a faded tenement she stopped.

It was not an apartment, but a single room, and there was an air of sadness about it. It was large enough and furnished adequately, but something seemed to be missing. She said she would make coffee. He asked her not to bother, but she went about getting things from a gloomy corner anyway. A moment later she stood rigid, crying softly, keeping her face tight so as not to cry aloud. After a while she turned, dabbing at her eyes with a tiny pink handkerchief.

"Forgive me. My mother died recently. It's hard to adjust to things like that."

He nodded, not knowing what to say.

"After father died she sold our house and we moved here, so I would be closer to school. She used most of the money for me, never went anywhere, never bought herself anything." She shrugged helplessly. "I don't think the results were worth the sacrifice."

"How old are you?" he asked.

Tired lines on her forehead robbed her of her youth. "I'll be twenty-three soon."

"That's a nice age," he said. "You're old enough to be a woman, and you're young enough to enjoy it."

She looked straight at him. "You don't understand! I didn't graduate! I had no right to be at that dance! I won't even be able to make it up!"

He said nothing for a moment, then, "I didn't graduate either."

She was surprised. He seemed so intelligent. "Why not?"

He smiled faintly. "The answer to that would involve a story."

"About what?"

"A man. . . ."

"What sort of man?"

"One who's dying before he's ready to."

"I'd like to hear about him," she said.

"He went to school here, an 'A' student, with a brilliant future in engineering." He tried to sound nonchalant, but it didn't come off well. "Then suddenly one night he woke from a dead sleep, gasping and gagging for air."

"What was wrong with him?"

"Cystic Fibrosis was the name of the villain. They told him he should be grateful for having lived so long because most victims died in adolescence. They told him he was living on borrowed time."

"Where is he now?"

"Oh, roaming around, visiting old places, trying to recapture a few memories."

"Has he been successful?"

He shook his head. "No, time and things have gone on, just as if he'd never existed."

131

"But that's not fair!" she cried. "He has no link with the past, and now he has no future. How meaningless his life has been."

"Meaningless, in this world perhaps. . . ."

She looked at him, knowing all along he had been speaking of himself. "You sure you're not a priest?"

He chuckled softly, and the mucous in his lungs came up to choke him. He covered his mouth with a handkerchief and shook with each wracking cough.

She spoke quickly and loudly, as if she didn't notice. "I think I'll go to night school! There's some money left. Perhaps I'll write a book. I can do it during the days and on weekends. . . ."

He stopped coughing and stood up. It was time to leave. "Will it be a good book?"

"Oh yes!" she said with inspiration. "It will be a beautiful book, about a foolish little girl who didn't know how fortunate she was, until a young man with the heart of a giant opened her eyes."

He took her hand and bowed, like he'd done at the dance, and softly kissed her shaking fingers. Then he went away, and though he would never return, they were both glad he had come back to this place.

THE REVOLUTION
THE REVOLUTION AND MISTER WILSON

by

Eugene (Samad) Watson

THE CELL WASN'T REALLY BIG ENOUGH FOR
one man, now sixteen were crammed into the five by seven
box. There wasn't enough room for them all to sit at the
same time, so half stood, while the others sat on the floor.
They talked in whispers and one grizzled character believed
they were going to be executed. The others thought him
mad. In a few days someone would stamp on this half-
baked uprising and they would be back in their homes.

"We're going to be exterminated," the grizzled man said,
"just like the Jews were in Nazi Germany."

Wilson told himself it was a joke, in poor damn taste,
but still only a joke. He told himself this, as they starved
him half to death, as they beat him whenever they felt the

133

compulsion to do so. He didn't realize that he'd been telling himself the same thing for more than a month now, that he had to tell himself something or his spirit couldn't survive. "'You're a damn fool!" he shouted at the grizzled man.

The others grew tense. They had been beaten for talking. They had been beaten for many reasons, some for no reason at all. No one said anything. No one even looked Wilson's way. Just before evening a little bald headed man was taken out. He came back a few hours later.

"What did they want?" Wilson asked.

"Did they beat you?" the grizzled man wanted to know.

The little man picked out a spot on the floor and stared dully at it. "They're going to kill us," he finally whispered.

"Bullshit!" Wilson snapped, and squeezed his way to the floor. The grizzled man grinned at him.

Two days later dark-faced Bantu's shoved them into a line of other prisoners, about fifty of them. The sun was not yet up and teeth began chattering up and down the line. A moment later a rack-bodied truck rattled into the prison yard and they were herded into the back. Three of the rebels, with automatic weapons, stationed themselves on the tailgate, while another sat on top of the cab.

They rode down Elizabeth Street, past Joubert Park and the University of Witwatersrand. Wilson's wife, Hattie, had been an assistant philosophy professor there and he thought about her for a moment, wondering what they had done with the women. Then, being honest with himself, he became more concerned about what they were going to do to him.

The truck turned off Elizabeth Street onto Main, heading north and out of the city. Bantu soldiers peered at them from behind sandbagged gun emplacements, their shiny black faces glistening with arrogance and a new awareness. A foot touched Wilson's and he saw that the grizzled man sat facing him, grinning sickly.

"They're going to kill us," someone down the line whimpered.

"Bullshit!" Wilson said irritably, and closed his eyes, finding a sort of peace in the rhythm of the swaying truck.

"Run!"

Incensed by the cry, several men scrambled for the sides of the truck. They died on the rack-body or in the street. The only one who reached the sidewalk was the little baldheaded man and a chattering machine gun jerked him to a stop in front of a little green picket fence. Fear numbed Wilson's mind, fear coupled with an intense hatred for the grizzled man. He was the one who had alarmed the others, yet he remained where he was with that evil smile plastered on his face. The truck started forward. No one bothered to pick up the corpses.

A mile or so more and they turned onto a dirt road, half grown over with vegetation. Between a thatched hut and a large square pit the truck creaked to a stip. Rifle butts menaced them into the hut and they were ordered to strip. While the others were taking off their clothes, Wilson peeked through a chink in the front wall of the hut. He saw Bantus and one man wearing khaki's, taller and darker than the rest. The rising sun glinted off a large golden ring in his ear.

"They're going to kill us," the grizzled man said, and began to cry. Naked, he was rail-thin and slatty. Wilson gave

135

him a contemptuous look and started pulling off his rumpled gray suit.

Bantu soldiers prodded them out, pushed dying men to their grave. Wilson was the first one into the hole, shoved by the press of prisoners behind him. The soldiers formed two lines around the pit. A brief pause followed, a moment of silence, when even the birds in the trees around the clearing grew still.

"Ready!" The command came from the earringed man, precise, confident, a little triumphant.

"Aim!"

"Fire!"

Bullets thudded into flesh, zinged off of stones, thwacked into the mud clay sides of the hole. Screeches and death wails were everywhere, as bodies danced wildly to the tune of M-14's and carbines. The grizzled man tumbled into Wilson and carried him down. Spittle from his dying mouth splotched red on Wilson's face and neck. The shooting stopped as abruptly as it had started and the earringed man moved forward, surveying the contents of the pit. A little mountain of men had been reduced to food for worms and maggots. The earringed man smiled faintly, but at the same time two tears slid down his ebony cheeks.

Wilson didn't move. Though the urge to blink his eyes was great, to blink meant to die, so he picked out an object and concentrated on it. He picked out the earring. Was it the mark of Bantu courage? Was it the badge of a chief? Was it the sign of the warrior who had slain the lion? Before he realized it, the need to know had overpowered all else and he rolled the grizzled man off of him.

136

Rifle bolts snapped on all sides, but a wave from the earringed man halted the soldiers' intentions. He squinted at Wilson, chalk-colored, blue-veined, streaked with someone else's blood, still plump though he hadn't been eating well. "Be brief. I have business with the living."

Wilson was amazed at his own calm. He was seconds from death, but the idea no longer terrified him. "Why the earring in your ear?"

The earringed man shrugged. "An earring belongs in the ear. It would look foolish anywhere else."

Wilson grinned at the reply. "Why the smile and the tears at the same time?"

"Perhaps the smile covers the tears," the earringed man said. "Perhaps the tears cover the smile."

Wilson nodded and laughed. "Why are we enemies?"

The earringed man wore a .45 on his hip. He unsnapped the holster. "Maybe the sun has made us enemies."

"Bullshit!" Wilson said, just before the bullet pushed his right eye through the back of his head.

An aide brought the earringed man a pair of sun glasses. He put them on and the tears stopped. As he scanned the tangle of human bodies, he wondered why the last man hadn't been afraid. "Bullshit!" he said finally, and turned away. "Shit!" he said, when another truck rumbled into the clearing.

A MAN CALLED CAIN

by

Frank Earl Andrews

THE TRAIN CAME FROM THE NORTH, STOPPING
at the junction only long enough to exchange a non-paying
passenger for a mail sack. He jumped from the last box car,
put down a small bundle and stretched cramped muscles.
He was a well proportioned young man and his khaki pants
and gray sweatshirt, though wrinkled, fit him nicely. He
cupped a hand over his eyes and looked south.

There were hills ahead of him, distinct and sharp. In
front of the hills was an ocean of grass, so great a man
could walk through it for days and be alone all the time.
More hills rose to the west, mountains this time, wearing
white snowcaps that shone like the tips of a giant ice cream
cones.

He had ridden a tractor and trailer going south, jumped
a train traveling through the mountains. He had passed
forests of cottonwoods and pines, gone through low, flat

country with miles between houses. He had crossed great swamps, rivers that roared out defiantly, streams that gurgled softly and trickled out of sight. There had been nights when the chill reached his bones and days when the sun burned him red. Now there was grass and trees and a fresh, new smell in the air. A man wouldn't be stifled out here.

Later on, when the sun left the sky, he moved into a sandy bottomed hollow and started a fire. After the twigs had crackled into flames he opened a can of beans and dumped them in a small pan. He was just getting ready to eat when a harsh voice broke through the normal sounds of night.

"Don't move, pal!" Four men walked into the circle of firelight. Two of them had guns in their hands.

"What do you want?"

Carney Thompson stepped forward, dust and wrinkles making a once immaculate silk suit appear shabby. He was a short man, stocky, with a hard square face and thick lips.

"Your name Cain?"

"No. . . . Horton. . . . Roger Horton."

"Where you headed . . . Horton?"

"No place special."

Frank Makins, youngest of the four spoke abruptly. "What're we waiting for? Kill him!"

On Roger's left side, Pogo Hardin, slender but hard, laughed. It was a hoarse cackle. "Scared, Frank?"

The firelight played over their faces, with Roger in the middle on his knees. It wasn't a good place to be. He didn't try to get up. They would kill him if he moved. He licked his lips nervously. "I've only got thirteen dollars."

"We ain't after money, pal."

"What do you want?"

"Some answers, and if you got good sense they'll be the right ones."

Roger nodded. His knees hurt. It wasn't right for a man to be on his knees this way. "Can I get up?"

Thompson nodded. "Don't try nothing stupid."

Roger rose, standing taller than anyone present. Behind him Eddie Cramer, evil faced and thin, went through his bundle.

"What are you doing here?" Carney Thompson asked.

Roger pointed south. "There's a small town behind the hills. I'm going there."

"Where'd you come from," Thompson wanted to know.

"Saint Charles."

"What about before that?"

"Chicago."

Frank Makins stiffened. Pogo Hardin moved his feet. Eddie Cramer stopped searching his pack. Carney Thompson regarded him steadily.

"How come you moved to Saint Charles?"

"I was sent to jail there."

"You sure you're not looking for somebody?"

"I'm not looking for anybody," Roger said, "just a place."

"What kind of place?"

"Somewhere I can fit in."

"If we told you to move on, would you?"

Frank Makins broke in suddenly, his face shiny with sweat and worry. "It's not safe to let him go! If he was Cain do you think he would admit it? Christ, did you think Madden was going to let us walk away with half a million dollars worth of his dope? We should have been back in Chicago with it four days . . ."

"Goddamnit!" Carney Thompson barked. "Will you shut your frigging face?" He turned back to Roger. "You know a guy named Charlie Madden?"

"Everybody in Illinois knows Charlie Madden," Roger replied.

Carney Thompson relaxed. "There'll be no killing. This guy ain't Cain."

"He ain't got no gun either," Eddie Cramer said. "He ain't got nothing but beans and bread."

Carney Thompson repeated his earlier question. "If we told you to move on, would you?"

Roger nodded.

"You can't let him go!" Makins persisted.

Carney ignored him. "That'd be your best bet," he said to Roger, "but just to make sure you don't renege maybe we better give you a sample of what's waiting if we should run into you again."

All four of them stepped closer. Roger looked quickly from one face to the other. Behind him the slide of an automatic snapped back. The sound was loud.

"Tie his hands with something."

"Like hell!" Roger lunged at Carney Thompson, but Pogo was faster and slapped him behind the ear with a .45. While he was shaking the cobwebs out of his head Eddie Cramer tied his hands with a belt. Frank Makins moved forward, fists raised. Roger stiffened in preparation, but the bone crunching fist drove him down on his knees. He rose under his own power and used his foot. Frank Makins screamed and backed up, hands clutching painfully

142

at his groin. But that didn't stop it and the blows came from every direction. Roger went down again, trying to fight away a wave of rapidly descending darkness. Then someone kicked him in the forehead and he fell into a bed with no sides, no bottom, no way of escape.

"Hold him up. Get him off of the ground."

They beat him for nearly an hour, until they were too tired to go on. Frank Makins leaned against Roger's pack, face wet, knuckles cut and bleeding. Eddie Cramer rested on his knees, saliva dribbling from the corners of his mouth. Pogo Hardin sat on the ground, his breath coming in huge gasps. Carney Thompson stood quietly nearby.

"Untie his hands."

Roger could not see the fire. He could not see the faces of the men who had beaten him or hear the sounds they made. A foot grated near his head and a knife passed through the leather holding his wrists. Carney Thompson looked at Frank Makins.

"Satisfied?"

Makins shrugged. "If he's Cain, it'll take more than that."

Carney sighed. "Spread his legs apart."

They rolled him over. Two of them held him by his legs. He stirred and through a red haze saw the barrel of a snub-nosed .38 gaping hungrily down at him. He twisted frantically, but a foot pinned his throat and choked him. Fire belched out of the gun twice and the lancing agony raced up his leg, his side, his chest. By the time it reached his brain he was unconscious.

"Get the car," Carney said to Makins.

Eddie Cramer nudged Roger with his foot. "If he's Cain, and he lives, he'll be after us."

Pogo breathed noisily. "If he's not Cain, and he's a man, he'll be after us anyway."

The sound of a car engine filled the night and the three men moved out of the hollow. Roger lay curled in a ball near the fire, the back of his shirt torn completely away. The car rumbled off and in a moment there was only the noise of the sputtering fire. In a little while that went out.

(2)

Whenever Fred Hartgrove had an important decision to make, he drove the jeep out across the valley, where the flat land stopped and the hills began. With a solid row of mountains in front of him, he turned and parked. As he looked out over all that was his, he felt like he was looking at his whole life. There were four peach orchards, so vast a man could get lost in them, acres of vegetables and five hundred purebred Herefords eating his grass. His home followed the line of ancient Texas hacienda's, warm during the savage snows of winter, cool in the smothering month of July.

He had been thinking about selling. It was because of Charlotte. One day he looked up and realized she was a woman. This was good country, with a lot of nice people, but he didn't think the right man for her was around here. It would be a waste if she didn't have a chance to select from among the best.

Away to the north he saw something move and stood up in the Jeep. There were no field workers this year and the Herefords were grazing in the south pasture. He wondered what a man might be doing on his land.

Charlotte was on the veranda when her father drove into the yard. He had a man in the back seat, with blood smearing his face and clothes.

"Ma! Ma!"

Esther Hartgrove appeared in the doorway. "What is it?"

"Pa. . . . He's got a man. . . . He might be dead. . . ."

Esther Hartgrove hurried back inside, to the downstairs bedroom, thinking quickly and coherently of everything she must do. She was turning back the covers on the bed when Charlotte and Fred half carried, half dragged, Roger in. They laid him on the bed and Fred felt for a pulse beat.

"He's still alive."

"Pa!" Charlotte cried. "Look at his leg!"

Fred touched Roger's blood-soaked thigh. He moved and a low moan escaped from his lips. Charlotte looked at the marks on his cheeks, around his eyes and nose. Esther Hartgrove went out and returned a few minutes later with a basin of hot water and some towels.

"His pants leg, Fred."

Fred Hartgrove ripped Roger's pants to the waist and tugged his shirt from under the khaki's. Charlotte drew off his shoes and socks. Esther Hartgrove dipped a cloth into the basin and began swabbing the red and blue bruises. When she got to his leg, caked with dried blood and dirt, she stopped and looked at her husband.

145

"He's been shot!"

"Maybe he was in a fight," Charlotte said. "Maybe . . ."

"A one-sided fight," Fred said. "His hands were tied. You can see the marks on his wrists."

"You mean someone tied him up and then beat him?" Charlotte asked with emotion.

"Only a guess," Fred Hartgrove said. "Only him and the people that done it knows what really happened."

Esther touched his leg and lines appeared on his forehead. A hand rose, then fell again.

"Easy, Ma. . . ."

"I think we should get a doctor," Esther suggested. "I'm afraid to do anything that might not be right."

Fred eased a towel under the wounded leg. "We'll have to call the sheriff too."

"Charlotte, empty this and fill it up with warm water. Bring more towels too."

Charlotte got the water and towels and as she sat them down she looked at his face again, dark against the white pillow case. She knew she would have to leave while they stripped off his shorts and went out to the veranda. She was just in time for the sunset, a sea of red gold, changing so slowly it looked like a painting. "Where did you come from?" she wondered aloud. No one in the house had ever seen him before. Her father knew everybody and would have mentioned it if he knew him. He had been tied up and beaten. She wondered what kind of people would do a thing like that to a man, and why.

Later that evening they sat in the high-ceilinged living room. A television commentator droned on about the desperate straits of the American economy, but no one paid any attention. "Doc can't make it till morning," Fred said. "I hope he doesn't take too long. That boy is hurt bad."

"Why don't you take him into town, Fred?"

"I don't think we should move him more than we have to."

"Did you call the sheriff?" Esther asked.

"Yes. Tom'll be out in the morning too."

"Why the sheriff, Ma? He didn't do anything wrong."

"We don't know that," Esther said. "He might be involved in something we shouldn't get mixed up in."

"He's in our house," Charlotte said. "We're already mixed up in it."

"We had no choice," Esther said. "But it doesn't make what happened to him any of our business."

Charlotte was insistent. "He's a human being, Ma. People have got to help each other when they're in trouble."

Esther had no answer for that. She smiled at her daughter and picked up some knitwork from an end table near her chair.

"Where do you think he come from, Pa?"

"At a guess, I'd say North."

"Maybe he was passing through and got in a fight."

"Maybe he's wanted by the police," Esther said. "Did you look in his pockets, Fred?"

"Yes. I had hoped to find out where he came from or who he was. He only had thirteen dollars."

"Do you think he'll go after those men, Pa?"

"How do you know it was more than one man?"

"Just something I thought about."

"We'll have to wait and see," Fred replied, wondering about that himself.

(3)

He was awake when she brought him a tray. He watched her come in. She was lovely, with hair just a shade darker than gold. She nodded without speaking and set down the tray.

"I'm not hungry," he said. His head hurt; his stomach ached; a steady pain throbbed in his left thigh; his mouth tasted of food and swallowed blood.

She uncovered the food anyway. "That doesn't mean you shouldn't eat."

"Miss . . . where am I?" He was curious, not hungry.

She was by the door, but she turned, carelessly brushing back a wisp of gold hair. "This is the Hartgrove place. We're twelve miles from Little Forks. I'm Charlotte Hartgrove."

The names meant nothing nor the distance from town. "How did I get here?"

She told him. He didn't remember that part. "You must have wandered this way on your own."

He nodded, but she did not leave and her green eyes were quizzical. "You were pretty bad, so we put you to bed."

"When was this?"

"Yesterday afternoon. Doc Collins was here early this morning and fixed your leg. Don't you remember?"

"Not too good."

She moved closer to the bed. Her face was clear and honest and when she looked at him her eyes were steady. She was a nice looking girl, one a man would be glad to be seen with.

148

"The sheriff will be here soon."

"What does he want?"

"Are you afraid of him?"

"I don't know him."

"He wants to know what happened. Can you tell him?"

"Yes . . . some of it."

"That's what he's coming for. He's the sheriff and it's his job to find out. You don't have to be afraid if it wasn't your fault."

"I'll tell him, Miss."

"The doctor doesn't like your leg. He says you may have trouble with it."

He didn't say anything and tiny lines of confusion wrinkled her forehead. "Aren't you worried about your leg?"

"I'm afraid to."

She understood and her forehead cleared. "Who shot you?"

"There were four of them. I don't know which one did it."

"Why did they do it?"

"I don't know. I never saw them before."

"They must have had a reason. . . ."

"They thought I was after them."

"Were you?"

"I told you. . . . I never saw them before."

"We talked about you last night. I said you might want to go after them."

"Will you?"

"Would you?"

"I don't know." He sounded angry, but he was entitled to be. "I think you should eat now. The sheriff will be here soon."

Fred Hartgrove was in the yard when Tom Fitch drove up in the red sheriff's van. "Hello, Tom."

"Fred." Tom Fitch climbed out, turning his head away from the bright sun. "You in any trouble out here?"

"No, just something we're not sure about. Young fellow got himself beat up and shot."

"How bad?"

"Not enough to kill him, but he'll know it."

Sheriff Fitch was a shaggy man in his fifties, but he knew his job and did it well. He took off his white Stetson and wiped the sweat from the band. "Could it have been an accident?"

"I don't think so. His hands were tied. You can see the marks on his wrists."

"Did he tell you anything?"

"I figured I'd best leave that to you."

The sheriff nodded and headed for the house. "Guess you better let me talk with him then."

The bedroom door was open when they came in. The sheriff eased his chunky frame into a leather-covered arm-chair near the foot of the bed. He crossed his legs and hooked the Stetson on his knee.

"I'm Sheriff Tom Fitch."

Roger had a pillow propped under his back. "Roger Horton." Fred Hartgrove stood by the door. Roger noticed the same features in both the man and his daughter. "I appreciate you helping me out."

"Glad I could," Fred said.

150

Sheriff Fitch leaned forward. "Suppose you tell us how it happened."

There wasn't much to tell and it didn't take long. The two men listened attentively while Roger told them everything, including the three years in Saint Charles. When he finished the sheriff sat back.

"You think they mistook you for this fellow, Cain?"

"At first they did."

"You say one of them mentioned drugs?"

"Yes . . . , like they were supposed to deliver it somewhere."

"To somebody in Chicago named Madden?"

"Yes."

"You know this Madden?"

"I know of him."

"What about the man called Cain?"

"He's a syndicate enforcer, but nobody knows what he looks like. They say he's killed over a hundred men."

Fred Hartgrove whistled through his teeth. "Sounds like a man to stay clear of."

"What it means then," the sheriff thought out loud, "is that they've never seen the man they're afraid of." He looked at Roger speculatively. "Wonder why they didn't kill you, just to be sure?"

"I promised to go somewhere else," Roger said, "but that was before they shot me."

The sheriff rose and put on his hat. "If I locate them I might need you for identification. You planning to stay around here?"

"Only until I can travel."

"Where you headed?"

"No particular place."

"What're you looking for?"

"A job, first . . ."

"You know anything about farming?"

"No, I've never been on a farm, until now."

"Well, maybe you'll find something around here," the sheriff said. "Go see Harry Wylie when you're able. I heard he was looking for help. Goodbye, Horton. Sorry you were hurt."

Fred Hartgrove remained in the doorway after the sheriff went out, then sat down. He regarded Roger for a moment. "How old are you, Roger?"

"Twenty."

"That's an interesting age, about the best age a man can be. You look like you been around a bit, on your own I mean."

"Since I was twelve."

"No family?"

"Not worth mentioning."

"It's about time to get settled down, ain't it? Find yourself something and stick with it?"

"That's what I want," Roger said.

"You sure you know what you want?"

"The last three years opened my eyes."

Fred Hartgrove shook his head. "Three years in jail. That's a nice chunk of living down the drain."

"It wasn't only the three years," Roger said. "It was the cons around me, guys my own age who will be old men before they see the streets again. Some of them won't ever see the outside at all. I want to make sure I don't die in a place like that."

"There's more to it than a job. A man needs a home, some things of his own that he can take pride in. He needs a good woman too, somebody he can talk to, somebody he'd be willing to die for."

"I know that."

"Then stop running so fast!" Fred punched a fist into his palm. "Slow down long enough to make sure you're not missing anything. Could be you've speeded right past what you're after."

Roger moved on the bed. "I don't know how I'm going to pay you back."

Fred scowled and stood up. "Maybe that jail didn't open your eyes wide enough. Everything ain't got a price on it. You stay in that bed until you're well enough to get out. It don't cost you nothing because it don't cost us nothing to be human. Eat your food." Fred went out. A moment later she came back, but only to close the door.

(4)

Roger got out of bed a week later. At the end of another week he rode with her. She drove the Jeep, handling it smoothly, as the wind brushed the hair back from her face. The air smelled of wood and green vegetation. When the road reached the top of a hump-backed hill she stopped.

"Down there is our biggest orchard. Over there are some of our Herefords."

He looked where she pointed. "I know you don't take care of a place this size by yourselves."

"No, we were using migrant workers from Mexico. No one could handle them but Pa. Last year he hurt his back

153

pretty bad and things just started running down. The Mexicans came this year, so we let them take what they wanted from the orchards and fields. . . ." She looked down quickly. "I think he's going to sell."

He was puzzled. "Why?"

She brushed a hand across her forehead, not sure she should discuss it with him. She finally decided he was only curious and it wouldn't hurt for him to know. "He doesn't think I know . . . and don't you tell him."

He glanced at her sharply. "Sorry. I wasn't being nosey."

"I know you weren't," she said quickly.

He looked out again at the rolling green countryside, bordered on two sides by majestic mountains. The sun made him squint. "A man dreams about a place like this. You're giving it up."

"I'm not giving anything up," she said shortly. "I don't want to leave . . . ever. . . . Besides, I'm not a man."

"Is that why your father's selling, because you're a woman?"

She nodded. "I heard him tell Ma it was time I started thinking about marriage. He thinks I should get a chance to meet more people, so he wants to move east. I wish I were a man."

"Don't wish you were anybody but you," he said.

"Why not? When you were in prison, didn't you wish you were someone else?"

"I used to think about things like that in Saint Charles, but even then I didn't want to be anybody else. Oh, it would be nice being the president of the United States, but it wouldn't be any good unless I was President Roger Horton. If I couldn't keep my own feelings and thoughts I wouldn't change places with a king." He grinned at her. "Besides, you wouldn't make as nice a man as you do a woman."

She blushed. "Why not?"

He felt that he had said too much already and changed the subject. "You won't have any trouble finding buyers."

"I'm glad you said that . . . about me not wishing I was anyobdy but myself. . . . I mean . . ."

He nodded. "You think we should look around some more?"

She knew he was trying to stay aloof, and why. "Which way?"

He grinned again. She thought it made him twice as handsome. "That's like the fish asking the cat how to swim. I'm the tourist; you're the guide."

She drove down a grassy slope and over a stream, on a bridge made out of tree trunks. On the other side she stopped. "This stream starts about three miles back in the hills. It's fed by an underground spring and never dries up. Pa built the bridge when I was a little girl."

He climbed out, grimacing when a hot needle stabbed his thigh. He knelt and drank deep of the cold mountain water. She watched the shirt tighten across his back, wondering if he would go after the men who had shot him.

"You've been thinking about it."

He straightened up. "Thinking about what?"

"Those men."

"Yes."

"What are you going to do?"

He shrugged his shoulders. "Nothing I can do, unless I see them again."

"You couldn't forget?"

He touched his leg. "No."

"They were afraid of you."

He looked straight at her. "Every man gets hurt sometime in his life, maybe more than once. If he knows why, he can stand it. If he's done something wrong, maybe he can forget it."

"They thought you were someone else."

"I *knew* I wasn't! That makes a difference! They knew it too, before they shot me!"

They rode back to the house in silence. She parked by the veranda and went inside. He stayed in the Jeep, his good leg slung over the side, trying to figure out why she went in without saying anything.

"Roger, supper's ready."

It was a strange feeling hearing Esther Hartgrove call his name like that. It was as if he belonged here. He wore another man's clothes, slept in his bed and was about to eat his food. What disturbed him most was that he had fallen in love with that same man's daughter.

Fred and his wife were at opposite ends of a long table. His seat was across from Charlotte. She had her hair tied back in a tight bun. It shone just the same. Esther Hartgrove passed him a plate of roast beef.

"How's your leg, Roger?"

"Not too bad."

Charlotte flashed him a quick glance.

"I'll have it looked at by Doc Collins before I leave."

Nobody said anything to that. Nobody said anything during the rest of the meal, until Esther Hartgrove poured coffee.

"You planning to look for those men?" Fred asked.

"Roger stared into his coffee cup. "I don't know where to look."

"If you did . . . ?"

Roger nodded. "I'd go after them."

"They have guns, Fred said.

"If I see them," Roger replied, "I'll get a gun."

"If you see them, boy," Fred warned, "you better *have* a gun. They won't wait for you to go and get one."

"I'll be leaving in the morning," Roger announced. He hadn't meant to be so abrupt. "I want to thank all of you for taking care of me."

Fred was the only one who looked at him. After a moment he got up and went into the living room. He came back carrying a short rifle. "You'll need a gun, but not a pistol. We got laws against a man carrying a pistol." He offered the rifle to Roger.

Roger slid back his chair and stood up. He took the rifle, hefted it, liked the feel of it in his hands. He'd never used a gun before. "I don't have much money."

"Didn't ask you for any," Fred grumbled. "I don't like seeing a young man so bitter. I don't hold with killing either, but sometimes it's the only way to get things settled."

They were all looking at him now and he could feel their concern. He knew they wanted him to stay and he also knew that another chance like this might be a long time coming. "I needed that leg," he mumbled, and limped from the room.

(5)

The black Lincoln sat concealed in a stand of pines, just north of Little Forks. Makins and Carney Thompson were in the front, with Pogo Hardin and Eddie Cramer huddled in the back. The freezing night air had no difficulty finding its way in, but Carney wouldn't let anyone use the heater. That meant running the engine and they were low on gas.

"Damn!" Pogo exclaimed. "It's colder than an Eskimo's snatch! How long we gonna sit here?"

"Until I decide to leave," Carney Thompson said. "We got half a tank of gas and two dollars between us."

"We got about a million in heroin," Cramer said.

"Yeah, sure," Carney said dryly. "We check into a motel and hand the manager a twenty dollar bag of horse."

"We would have had some money, if it wasn't for creep face." Pogo looked at the back of Frank Makins' head.

Makins twisted around. "Who the hell you calling . . ." He started over the seat.

Carney grabbed him roughly by the shoulders and pulled him back down. "Shit!" he cursed. "You couldn't even take off a super market; now you want to be big time killers."

"Don't try to shift it on anybody else," Pogo said. "You know who messed it up."

"What did you want me to do with the old punk?" Makins cried. "Kiss his wrinkled ass? He was coming at me!"

"No sense crying about it now," Carney said disgustedly. "Let's concentrate on the bank in Little Forks."

Eddie Cramer spoke suddenly. "When *are* we going to take off the bank in Little Forks? It's been two weeks since

158

the Austin joke. If we ain't cooled off by now, we never will be."

"Got me wondering too," Pogo said. "The original plan was to take off Madden's dope, get some expense money and head for Mexico. We ain't done nothing but beat up a kid, blow a stick-up, and sit on a mountain picking our noses."

"Same plan as before," Carney said. "We hit the bank, drive into the hills, ditch the car and cross the river on foot."

Pogo was persistent. "When?"

"When I say so."

Cramer had a distant look on his face. "Why did we beat up that kid?" he asked from out of the blue.

"We hurt him bad," Pogo said.

"He won't forget it," Carney agreed, "if he's alive."

"He said his name was Horton," Pogo said.

"So what?" Carney wanted to know.

"I mean he wasn't Cain."

"You ever see Cain?"

Pogo shook his head.

"How do you know then?"

"Did you ever see Cain?" Pogo countered.

"It was Cain," Makins said, before Carney could reply. "You didn't expect him to come wheeling up in a Rolls Royce, did you? He's smart, and traveling like a tramp is just the kind of trick he'd pull. You know his reputation."

Pogo thought about almost everything Makins had done since they'd taken off Charlie Madden's swag. He couldn't think of one thing he liked. "Been a lot of funny stuff going on."

"I'll spell it out plain for you," Carney said evenly. "Whoever he was, if he's after us, he won't be moving too fast, not with two bullet holes in his leg. If he's dead, we don't have to worry about him."

"Suppose he ain't Cain?" Pogo asked. "Suppose he ain't dead and he's the kind of guy who can't make himself forget something like that?"

"We got two men after us," Carney thought, but didn't say it. He didn't like the way the conversation had turned either. When he did speak his voice was controlled. "Ain't no chains on you, Pogo. Move out any time you like."

"That's what I had in mind," Pogo said softly, "after we split up the goodies."

The others stared. This was a good thing to know, a good thing for everybody to know. Eddie Cramer was the only one close enough to see the .45 Pogo held between his knees.

"I think we should move in the morning," Pogo said.

Eddie Cramer concurred, "Me too."

"Let's get it over with," Makins said.

Carney held his temper, wondering why Makins went along with Pogo and Cramer. In fact, he wondered why Makins opened his goddamned mouth at all. He was angry, but gave in. "Two of us'll go in ahead, check things out, make sure it's as easy as it looks."

"I'll go," Cramer offered.

"Me too," Pogo said. "What do we do when we get inside?"

Makins spoke quickly. "You and me cover the door. Eddie and Carney can get the money."

Pogo didn't like it, neither did the others, but nobody said anything. They settled down to sleep then, except for Carney Thompson, who stared out the window into the inky night and thought about the three men with him, punks who would mess up a wet dream. When the dawn pushed away the night he was still thinking about them.

(6)

The sun was not yet up, but the sky was clear, the air cool and with only a slight breeze. Roger stood in the yard, looking back at the house. He didn't want to leave, yet there were some things a man had to do whether he wanted to or not. Fred Hartgrove walked out on the long veranda.

"Knew you planned to go," Fred said. "Didn't think it'd be before breakfast."

Roger looked away. "Seemed like the best time."

Fred watched a feather of dust whirlwind up nearby, then drift quietly away. "I've always been proud of this place," he said. "Lately I've been wondering why. I got fruit and vegetables going to waste, livestock that needs to be fed, fences that need mending. Everywhere I look I can see something that should be done and I feel a pain because nobody's doing it. It's like maybe my arm's broke and nobody's trying to fix it. This place is my life, not just ownership, but my sweat and blood. I'm letting it die. . . ."

Roger understood. "Sort of like committing suicide."

"Hurt my back last year," Fred went on. "Never healed right and it hurts pretty bad sometimes. I couldn't find no-

161

body to keep things organized, so I laid off all the help. I was thinking about selling. Trouble now is, I'm not so sure."

"You don't want to sell," Roger said. It was a statement.

"You're not as old as I am," Fred Hartgrove said.

Roger stared at him. "You drive that Jeep. You walk to it and climb in. You're not that old."

"A good man might make it work."

"Hire somebody," Roger said. "If you don't like him, fire him and hire somebody else. Keep going until you find the kind of man you want.

"Could be I've found him."

Roger rubbed a hand across his face. "You offering me a job?"

"You want work. I need a good man."

"You don't know me. All you know is that I been in jail, that I've been beaten and shot."

"I know more about you than I would a complete stranger," Fred said. "I know how you look, partly what you want, and how you feel."

Roger wasn't sure. "I don't know much about farm work. I don't know if I can handle men, especially Mexicans."

"Many of the workers speak English."

Roger nodded. There wasn't anything else to think about. "If you're willing to take the chance. . . ."

"You don't rate yourself high enough, boy," Fred said. "Could be you're the one taking the chance."

Later in the day Roger worked in the garage, loading tools and wire into a pick-up truck. His thoughts were on the Hartgroves, mostly Charlotte, until he picked up a twenty-five pound sledge and his leg caved in. Then he thought about the fact that he was a cripple and about the four men who made him that way.

"Are you going to like it here?"

Roger looked up. He hadn't heard her come in. "I think so."

She stared at a wet spot on his Levi's. "Did Pa say anything about selling?"

"He talked about it."

"Will he?"

"I don't know."

"Roger, will he sell?"

He noticed the use of his first name. "I told him I wouldn't."

This pleased her and she didn't say anything more about it. The wet spot had grown bigger and his indifference to it angered her. "You should still be in bed."

"Yes, Miss," Roger said, and climbed into the truck.

She watched the truck move out of the yard and even after it was out of sight she looked in the direction it had gone. He was a stubborn man, but tall and good looking.

(7)

The next morning Roger had the truck in the yard early. The rifle was on the back shelf. Fred Hartgrove and his daughter came out and climbed in beside him, with Charlotte in the middle. When Esther Hartgrove waved from the veranda, part of her goodbye was for him.

"You drink beer, Roger?" Fred asked.

"A little." The road leading to the highway followed the contours of the land, crossing a stream, skirting boulders, weaving through green-leaved trees.

Fred laughed. "What about you, girl? You want a beer?" He ruffled her hair.

"Oh, Pa. . . ." Charlotte scolded. She brushed her hair with her hand. "You know how hard it is to keep my hair fixed."

The movement caused her thigh to brush Roger's. He looked at her and she flushed. Fred Hartgrove saw what was going on between them. He liked it.

Fred wanted to go to the bank first, but it wasn't open, so he decided to go up and annoy Doc Collins for a while. Charlotte went shopping for clothes and Roger went to Orville's, a community market that sold everything from hubcaps to corn flakes.

"I've changed my mind, Harvey," Fred told a sleepy Doc Collins. "I'm not selling. I came in to tell Harold Troxell."

"Glad to hear it," Doc grumbled, still in his pajamas. "That why you got me out of bed?"

Fred chuckled. "No, I want to know about Roger Horton, his leg . . ."

"It'll be stiff for a while," Doc said. "One of the bullets chipped a bone. If he lets it heal properly, he'll only have a slight limp."

Fred leaned back in his chair, his face reflecting a deep satisfaction. Doc squinted at him. "You look like the cat that just swallowed the mouse. How come you're so smug?"

"Not sure yet," Fred replied. "It'll take some time to find out."

"Whatever it is . . ." The sound of muffled gunfire downstairs brought them both to their feet.

Old man Orville noticed the rifle Roger carried. "Fred Hartgrove's, ain't it?"

"He gave it to me."

The wintry storeowner gave Roger a cursory once over. "He must think an awful lot of you."

"Why?"

"To let you have that gun. Japanese sniper rifle, ain't it?"

Roger shook his head. "I don't know."

"He took it off the Jap that killed his younger brother. They gave him a Silver Star."

Roger touched the polished stock. "I didn't know."

Orville plopped a box of 30-30 shells on the counter. "These fit like they was made for it."

"How much do I owe you?" Roger asked.

"You staying with Fred Hartgrove?"

"Yes, I took a job."

"Then your credit's good till you prove it ain't," Orville said. "Pay me next time you get in."

Roger started to protest, but two rolling shots shattered his intent. He raced outside, making it just in time to see the Lincoln squealing away from the bank. It was them! He couldn't see their faces or how many men were in the car, but he knew it was them. He pointed the rifle at the retreating auto and pulled the trigger. The dull click that greeted his ears was like a slap in the mouth. He'd forgotten to load the damn thing.

Pogo waited under the awning of a hardware store, across the town's single street from the bank. A white pick-up truck sat parked in front of the old, two-story, red-brick building. Two men had opened the bank twenty minutes ago, but the truck had been there before that. Wooden steps ran up the side of the building, so the top floor didn't belong to the bank. Maybe the truck owner was on the second flood. There wasn't much else to think about, except the sheriff's office one block down. Pogo crossed the street and moved under the stairs. A few minutes later he saw Eddie Cramer in front of the hardware store.

Makins and Carney came in slowly. Several stores were open, but no one was in sight. Makins stopped in front of the white truck and they climbed out, letting the motor idle. Pogo and Cramer sauntered over and they all stepped into the bank.

A long counter, topped with a high wire grille, dominated one half of the room. On the right, a railed-off section enclosed a desk and two chairs. Carney walked up to the teller's cage. Cramer moved to the desk. Makins closed the door and went to the left. Pogo stood on the right. Carney pushed his gun through the cage opening.

"Don't move, and keep your face shut!" Carney barked at John Leslie. Harold Troxell looked up from his desk. He opened his mouth to say something, but closed it when he saw Eddie Cramer's .38 pointed at his chest.

"Put your hands on your head and keep them there," Cramer told the bank manager.

"Open the cage!" Carney ordered the cashier. John Leslie looked nervously at Harold Troxell. "Don't give them any trouble, John."

John Leslie opened the cage door and backed up against the wall. Carney moved to the safe. It was open. He stuffed several bundles of money into two canvas sacks and backed out. Makins held the front door open for him and Cramer. When Pogo turned to follow, his eyes met Makins'. One thought reached out and welded the two men together.

"Frank!"

Pogo knew and dropped to the floor, his own gun spitting fire. In the space of a heartbeat, two loud roars filled the room and reverberated off the walls. No one noticed as John Leslie gasped and clutched at his chest. By the time Pogo dove into the back seat, Makins had the Lincoln screeching away from the curb.

The two-toned MG came from the north. The face of the man driving, beneath a carefully brushed Afro, was long and serious. He missed little as he rode, yet barely moved his head. The hands that held the wheel were smooth and well manicured. Just outside of Little Forks, he stopped at a roadside inn and went inside.

The tavern was long, low, and empty, except for a burly, red-faced bartender. He made no effort to conceal his distaste for the Negro. The brown-skinned man smiled faintly and put two one hundred dollar bills on the counter.

"You want these?"

The bartender reappraised the black man on the other side of the counter. This second scrutiny made him cautious. He nodded.

"Tell me something," the brown-skinned man said. "You get many visitors in this town?"

167

Before the bartender could answer, two loud explosions broke the morning calm. "What the hell!" he exclaimed, and rushed outside.

The black man took his time. He took out his billfold and carefully replaced the two one hundred dollar bills, then walked leisurely outside. He was in time to see the tail-end of the Lincoln disappearing behind a low hill. Four men in a Lincoln . . . four men, headed south. . . .

"You got visitors today," he said casually to the bartender, and started up the street toward the bank.

(8)

Little Forks came alive with hurried motion and people ran toward the bank from every direction. Harold Troxell appeared in the doorway, waving his arms frantically. "Get Doc Collins, quick!" he shouted. "John Leslie's been shot!"

A few minutes later Sheriff Fitch shouldered his way through the crowd. Fred Hartgrove sat on the floor of the cage, with John Leslie's head in his lap, while Doc Collins worked on the cashier's bleeding chest. Doc looked up at the sheriff and shook his head.

"His lung's tore all to hell," the old medic said.

The lawman listened to Harold Troxell's hurried explanation, then strode outside. "The bank's been robbed," he announced. "John Leslie's dead. Anybody that wants to help, wait in front of my office. The rest of you finish what you were doing."

168

People scattered every which way, until only two men remained, Roger Horton and the brown-skinned man. The sheriff motioned to Roger. "Troxell's identification of the hold-up men matches the description of the men who shot you." The sheriff took note of the rfle. He recognized it. "Troxell's pretty shook up, so you'll have to come along in case we need somebody to identify them."

Roger nodded and the sheriff started for his office. He brushed past the brown-skinned man, then stopped. "Who are you?"

"Name's Cain."

Tom Fitch remembered Horton's account of the man. He frowned. "You don't have anything to do with this."

"Not with the bank," Cain said quietly. "Just with the men who stuck it up."

"Except for the law, Roger Horton's the only one with an interest."

"Then there's three of us," Cain said in the same quiet tone. "The law, Roger Horton, and me. . . ."

Cars and trucks were beginning to congest in front of Tom Fitch's office. "Hell!" he said impatiently. "I ain't got time to stand here blabbing with you. If you want to come, I can't stop you."

Roger waited by the truck. Fred Hartgrove touched his arm. He tightened his hand on the rifle stock. "I got to have a gun."

"I'm not taking it from you," Fred assured him.

"I'll take care of it."

"Take care of yourself," Fred said softly.

Charlotte ran up, all out of breath. Roger looked at her, liking the way she fitted naturally into jeans and a shirt. "I don't want you to go, Roger!" she cried. "They know you! They'll kill you first!"

"I have to go. . . ."

"No! If you . . ." Fred took her arm. "Just make sure you come back," she said, almost pleadingly, and walked away with her father.

Roger watched her go, wondering when it had started with them, maybe even before Saint Charles. She'd been here in this land waiting for him, like the peach blossoms or the elusive silver streams. She knew what living was, and what to expect from it. . . .

"You're name Horton?"

Roger shook himself. It was the brown-skinned man he'd seen in front of the bank. "I don't know you."

"My name's Cain. Mind if I ride with you?"

The effect was like a douche of cold water. Roger had never expected a black man. He hesitated.

"The color of my skin have anything to do with your reluctance?" Cain asked.

Roger grew angry. "The proverbial crutch of the black man," he said. "It's not your color that bothers me. It's the business you're in."

"You haven't said yes or no."

Roger stared at the smooth, brown face, especially the eyes—slits that revealed nothing. He was the first to look away. "Unless you try to hurt me, you're the same as any other man."

The road south of Little Forks wove through the gaunt terrain, breasting low hills, rounding mountains and outcroppings. They hadn't gone more than thirty miles before the calvacade halted. Tom Fitch stood in the middle of the road. Roger walked up beside him.

"My authority stops here," the sheriff said, slapping his leg in irritation.

"County lines don't mean anything to me," Roger said.

"No, I guess they don't," Tom Fitch agreed. "Word's been sent ahead, so if they keep heading south they'll run into Sheriff Falls and his men. If they get past them there's still the border patrol." The lawman climbed back into the county van and made a U-turn. He pulled even with Roger, noticing the black killer still by Fred Hartgrove's truck. "The federal people have been alerted, so I guess we'll be hearing from Houston pretty soon." The last was for Cain, who knew it, but didn't change his expression.

Roger watched the vehicles turning back toward Little Forks, except for a rusty rack-bodied truck and six farmers with shotguns. Cain took out a pack of filter-tipped cigarettes. Roger declined one and he smoked. "What are your plans?"

"To catch them and kill them. That's all."

"How come you're so hot for these guys?" Cain asked.

"They tied my hands and beat me," Roger said. "They left a lot of marks."

"I don't see any marks."

"You can't see Tibet either," Roger said, but it's there." He looked south. "They thought I was you."

"They made a mistake."

"One too many," Roger said.

Cain blew out a thin trail of smoke. "I'd say you were the kind of man who held a grudge for a long time."

"You talk a lot, for a big-time killer," Roger said, and limped to the truck, wincing with every step.

(9)

From atop a flat-edged rock Eddie Cramer watched the search party turning around. He slid down. "They've stopped. We're okay in the rear. They left some men in case we try to double back."

Carney heard, but his attention was on Frank Makins and Pogo Hardin. "Who used his gun first?"

Makins watched Carney and Pogo carefully. "I did."

Carney stepped closer. "Why?"

Makins shrugged. Carney grabbed his face in one huge paw and squeezed. Makins colored, but made no move for his gun. Carney pushed him away and turned his back. Pogo waited, his suit jacket open, the butt of the .45 visible in his belt. Carney wanted to kill him, but they couldn't afford any shooting right now.

"There were two shots, Pogo."

Pogo was not afraid. "It was a stick up, wasn't it? I thought I had to shoot and I did. A lot of talking don't change it."

Carney stepped back. "Eddie, split the money and the snow."

Cramer moved to the two canvas sacks and a black valise. He dumped the money on the ground and counted it. When he was finished there were four piles of fifty-six

172

hundred dollars each. He took four plastic bags from the valise and put one beside each pile. He picked up his share and stepped back. Pogo and Makins did the same.

"If you stick, I give the orders," Carney said. "If you want to cut out, you can go any time after dark." He glanced at the Lincoln, partially concealed under a wide granite ledge. It wouldn't be hard to find, but there was nothing else they could do with it. "All right, let's go."

(10)

Roger almost drove past the spot where the Lincoln had turned off, but Cain touched his arm. The black gunman reached the car first, opened the door and felt the seat. It was cold. He lit a cigarette and looked around.

"Your life been hard?"

Roger had to think about that. "I always got enough to eat."

"Why make it hard?"

Roger wondered what he was getting at. "What do you mean?"

"Two men on a mountain, chasing four," Cain said. "If we catch them we'll kill them. They won't like that, so they'll try to kill us. Chances are they will. You're taking a big risk for a small reason."

"How come you're so concerned about me?"

"I'm looking out for you," Cain said, and started walking.

A deep crack opened into a canyon of whitened rocks. Light shone on the western side of the cliffs, blinding anyone who looked that way. Cain scanned the slits, look-

ing for a shadow that moved, listening for the fall of loose
stones. A plane whined by overhead, swung back low to
inspect them, then moved on again.

"You seem like a nice guy, Roger," Cain said. "I don't
suppose you ever thought much about it."

"What's your point?" Roger asked.

"I want you to let me kill those men."

"No!"

They rounded a curve and saw the four men. Carney
Thompson was the first to act. "Break it up. . . . Scatter.
. . ." They scrambled for cover, except for Eddie Cramer,
who dropped in his tracks. Pogo Hardin shouted his anger.
"Goddamn it! I told you we wasn't clear!"

A bullet whined past Roger's head. Cain pulled him
behind a knee-high boulder. "Give me your rifle."

Roger moved the bolt. "You got a gun."

"The distance is too far. I need that rifle."

Roger peered around the rock. "You don't need this
rifle."

Cramer sized up the situation immediately. Only a fool
would believe two men had come after four. It was a slick
trick, going back, then coming up again. While these two
drew the fire the others were moving into position along
the cliffs. But if he could make it to the end of the canyon,
where they'd come in at, he would be clear. Nobody'd
waste time coming after one man. He jumped up and started running.

Roger and Cain stood up together. "Wait until he's in
front of you," Cain hissed. "Lead him. . . ."

Roger hadn't considered that. He was getting ready to
kill a man and hadn't even thought of the proper way to do

174

it. He squinted along the barrel and waited for the running man to cross in front of the sight. When he did he pulled the trigger and the report blotted out all other sounds, rolling slowly away in a spreading echo. A pinch of dust spurted up fifteen feet behind Eddie Cramer.

Cain snatched the rifle out of Roger's hands and leaped atop the rock. He snapped the bolt, stood straight for a long second, then squeezed the trigger.

Cramer was on his stomach before he heard the explosion from the bullet that shattered his shoulder bone. He'd never been on the ground before, not like this, and everything seemed different, the dirt, the sky, the cliffs glowering down from both sides. Cain's shadow fell across his shaking form.

"Get up! A man should take it standing up!"

Fear moved in Cramer's stomach, where the money and heroin pressed against his flesh. Spittle from his mouth dribbled off his chin and dried up instantly in the parched sand. His face was scratched and bleeding, his shoulder numb with pain. He risked a sideways glance. His .38 lay only a few inches away. He could make it, if he rolled and fired. The only thing standing between him and freedom was a nigger.

He drew up his legs slowly, swaying on his elbows, then snatched the gun and rolled. . . . Cain's brown hands worked like mechanisms: firing and snapping the bolt, firing and snapping the bolt. The bullets ripped into Cramer's throat and chest, skidding him headfirst into a rock. Then he lay still.

Roger climbed down. "Why'd you do it?"

"Kill him?" Cain pulled a canvas sack out of Cramer's shirt.

"Take my gun. . . ."

"You don't know how to use it."

"I didn't get much of a chance."

"It was time for speed," Cain said, handing the sack to Roger. "If I need it again, I'll take it the same way."

"Why'd you give the money to me?" Roger was angry.

Cain stuffed the packet of heroin in his jacket. "I got what I came for." His eyes roved about the canyon. "What about the other three?"

"They've gone," Roger said.

Cain started off. Roger hesitated, then caught up. "If you take my gun again, I'll kill you." The black man from Chicago laughed until Roger's ears turned red. "What's so damn funny?"

"If I had your gun," Cain roared, "how would you kill me?"

When they stopped again the sun was nearly gone. Cain moved under a ledge and smoked. Roger knelt on his good leg a few feet away. "How long before we catch them?"

"You tired?"

"I was thinking about Fred Hartgrove."

"Why don't you go back?"

"No!"

"That his daughter I saw you with?"

"It's not what you think."

Cain laughed. "You're sure stuck on her."

"You don't know everything." Roger didn't know how much longer he could take the black killer and his superior manner.

176

Cain studied a niche in the rocks. "What I don't know, you can put in a thimble."

"Does killing make you feel like God?" Roger asked.

Cain answered indifferently. "I don't know. How does God feel when he kills a man?"

"Why are you a professional killer?" Roger pressed.

Clain flicked the ashes off his cigarette. "The pay's good and I got tired of fighting rats and roaches for my meals."

Roger was surprised. It was the first bit of emotion Cain had shown. "There's no justification in killing for money."

Cain looked at the tip of his cigarette. "It's not what a man does that determines right or wrong. It's whether he gets away with it or not."

"The men we're after didn't do anything to you," Roger reasoned.

Cain looked at the sky. The gray umbrella of night had closed in. "I never missed on a hit yet."

"A hit."

"A contract to kill a man."

Roger was incredulous. "You think that's a better reason than mine?"

Cain threw his cigarette out into the night. "To me it is. I'm a professional, like an artist or an actor."

"Killing doesn't take talent."

"Death rows all over the country are filled up with people who had no talent," Cain said.

"The FBI won't let you take the heroin back to Charlie Madden," Roger said.

Cain changed the subject. "We're not doing bad for city boys. Here we are, in the middle of nowhere, hot on the trail of our prey."

"You make it sound like we're hunting animals."

"Couldn't phrase it better myself."

The black man's smugness continued to irritate Roger. "Well, it's no game to me," he said sharply. "I don't like killing, but they made me a cripple. I didn't deserve it and they knew it. That's the reason *I'm* going to kill them."

"We'll see," Cain said quietly.

"Just stay out of my way," Roger warned.

Cain laughed. "Yassa, boss man."

(11)

In the hills further south the three men rested inside a small cave. Even though it was dark, they could still hear the sounds of a search plane, soaring high, dipping low, circling. Carney Thompson stood near the entrance. Frank Makins sat on the ground, rubbing his .45 on his shirt sleeve. Pogo Hardin squatted in a corner, his thin face gaunt, his eyes a little too bright.

"When the hell we gonna get out of these mountains?"

Carney didn't try to conceal his contempt. "Shut up! You been running off at the jibs ever since we left the bank."

"I got something to say and I'll say it!" Pogo said shrilly.

Carney didn't turn around. "Thought you was going to head out on your own?"

"And run into the cops?"

Makins blew dust out of his gun barrel, making a lot of noise while he did it. "There ain't no cops behind us."

Pogo glared. "Who the hell was we shooting at then? Who the hell was shooting at Cramer?"

Makins leaned forward, arms hanging loosely over his knees, his .45 dangling by the trigger guard. "The guy we beat up and a nigger."

"Who's the shine?"

Makins curled his lips. He wondered why he ever considered Pogo dangerous. "You know who it is. They don't have nigger cops in Texas."

Pogo scratched his head. "I never thought of that," he said dully. "What about Cramer?"

Makins grinned. He could kill Pogo now and nobody would say a word. "He might be in bed with a big-assed woman."

"He might be dead too!"

Makins didn't say anything to that. He started polishing the .45 again. "Why don't you try it on your own, Pogo?" he baited. "You could head west and lose yourself in the hills."

"Not me!" Pogo's voice was shaky. "Cramer's dead!" Nobody contradicted him. Cramer might be dead or sitting in a bar with a cold beer in his hand. "Cramer's dead!" he said again. "And we got a nigger named Cain after us. Jesus Christ! A black torpedo!"

Frank Makins was enjoying Pogo's terror. He was glad he'd missed at the bank. "Maybe Charlie Madden's an equal opportunity employer."

(12)

Dawn came quickly, slate gray and streaked with gold. As they moved down the side of a steep hill, Roger studied the ground. He saw nothing, no scuff marks, no shoe prints, no bent shrubbery, no indication that anyone had passed this way. "I think we lost them."

Cain shook his head. "I can see them."

Roger looked at the distant hills. "It was a while before he could pick out three vague dots moving between two peaks. Cain stopped. "We'll take a breather here."

All day long Roger's leg had been throbbing and several times he felt warm blood trickling down his thigh. He sat down on a large rock. "How come we're stopping?"

"We know where they are." Cain said calmly.

Roger wished there was some way to shake the black killer's composure. "You're not God!" It came out sudden and for no apparent reason.

Unruffled, Cain folded his arms and leaned against a towering boulder. "You keep mentioning God. He can't kill any better."

"Maybe not," Roger said, "but he's only taking back something he gave. You don't give anybody anything."

"It don't matter how a man dies," Cain said. "The end result is always the same."

"You're worse than the men we're after!" Roger blurted.

Cain looked hard at Roger. His words carried a warning. "You had best stop jigging at me, white boy."

Roger stared back. "I'm not afraid of you." He stood up. "You can rest if you want to. I'm going on."

Cain shrugged. "Go ahead."

The sun, so bright a moment before, had disappeared behind a wall of rolling black clouds. When the wind started whipping at Roger's bared head and blew sand in his face, Cain laughed that laugh of his. When the lightning exploded in the air and the rain drove Roger to shelter, Cain almost had convulsions.

"Rain rythmes Cain." Roger heard the black man's wild laughter. He couldn't see him because sheets of water made vision impossible for more than a few feet. "Cain rhymes with insane," he thought, and for the first time in his life he was afraid.

(13)

Carney, Pogo and Makins, stood with their backs to a granite wall, watching the rain drench a farmhouse below. An unpaved road snaked between the house and a barn and curved out toward the highway two miles south. A man came out of the house and went into the barn. A few minutes later he returned to the house.

"What about something to eat?" Pogo used a handkerchief to wipe rivulets of water from his face.

Carney hunched his shoulders against the downpour. "We won't have time."

Frank Makins shivered and crowded closer to the cliff. "Something hot would be nice."

Carney thought about it. "Maybe some coffee." Light came on in the windows, yellow light that bespoke of warmth and comfort. "I'll go down first. You two move behind the barn and wait until I call you."

Carney made a wide circle, head bent against the icy torrent, and came out on a porch in front of the house. The door opened before he could knock and a young man peered cautiously out. Carney grinned disarmingly. "I was wondering if I could borrow your phone. My car's in a ditch down the road. I think I made a wrong turn somewhere . . ."

The young man smiled with embarrassment. "We don't have a phone. My dad is old fashioned about things like that. He says the only time they ring is when somebody's taking a bath." He suddenly remembered his manners and swung the door wide. "Please come in."

Carney stepped inside. Water from his clothes dripped onto the thick green carpet. A woman sat in front of a television. She rose and flicked off the set. The young man closed the door.

"Where were you headed? There's nothing out this way but mountains."

"Uh . . . Little Forks. I should've been there yesterday."

"I guess you did make a wrong turn!" the woman said. "You're about sixty miles off."

"What?" Carney wondered if he sounded convincing.

"At least sixty miles," the young man said. "Maybe it's good you didn't get there."

"Why's that?"

"The bank was held up," the woman said. "One man was killed."

Carney cursed Pogo and Frank under his breath. Now they had two murders on them. "Did they get the ones that did it?"

"No, but Sheriff Falls says they're trapped in the hills,"

the young man said. "The roads are blocked and the Border Patrol's been alerted."

"Is the border near here?"

"About two miles," the young man replied.

"Chuck, let him sit down," the woman scolded gently. "I'll make some coffee."

Carney nodded his thanks and the woman went into the kitchen. Chuck moved to a sofa, motioning Carney to join him, but the stranger didn't move. Chuck thought it was because of his clothes, soaked, covered with mud and grime. "Soon as we get something hot in you, I'll lend you some things to wear. Nothing fancy, but at least you'll be dry."

"Thanks," Carney said. "You people live out here alone?"

"Except for my dad," Chuck answered. "But he's visiting in El Paso."

Carney needed to know no more and pulled out his .38. "Do what you're told and nobody gets hurt." Chuck's eyes opened wide. The woman came out of the kitchen. She stopped when she saw the gun. "If there's somebody you haven't told me about," Carney warned, "she gets it first."

"We're alone," Chuck said.

Carney backed to the front door and opened it. "Frank! Pogo!"

They came in through the kitchen. Makins shook himself. "They got a car?"

Carney closed the front door and leaned against it. "Probably in the barn."

"You can't use the car," the woman protested.

"You planning to stop us?" Carney asked.

"No. . . , but . . ."

"Then keep your mouth shut."

Pogo leered at the woman. She was young and pretty and had big legs. He liked broads with big legs. "Whatcha got to eat, lady?"

The woman glanced at her husband. "Eggs. . . . Roast beef . . ."

Pogo laughed loudly. "Fry up some eggs, baby. "I'm starved."

Chuck watched the three men carefully. They had killed already and would probably kill him and his wife. He had a shotgun, but it was in the bedroom behind the door. The shells were in the dresser. His wife went into the kitchen and Pogo followed her.

"My wife . . . I'll help. . . ."

"Stay where you're at!" Makins ordered.

Chuck took a faltering step toward the kitchen, then lunged suddenly for the bedroom. It was a foolish move because no man can outrun a bullet. Frank Makins shot him between the shoulder blades. The woman burst into the living room and swooned at the sight of her husband. She recovered and knelt on the floor beside him.

"What the fuck!" Carney said through clenched teeth. "Are you trigger happy?"

"Christ! You were standing there!" Makins argued. "He wouldn't stay put!"

Carney went to a window. He couldn't see anything. He wondered why the woman didn't cry. She was supposed to be crying. "Bring the car around front."

"What about her?" Makins asked. "She can identify us."

"Half of Texas can identify us," Carney said sourly.

"She'll be on the phone before we get a mile."

"They don't have a phone."

"You checked?"

"I said no!"

"We should kill her," Makins said.

"Is that all you know?" Carney asked tiredly.

"It solves most problems."

"You're a problem, Frank," Carney said softly. "Maybe somebody'll solve you pretty soon."

Makins turned away and moved over the woman. "Give me the car keys." She didn't look up, but fumbled through Chuck's pockets. After she handed the keys to Makins he went out.

The room filled with the odor of burning food and Pogo returned to the kitchen. Carney stayed with the woman and her husband. She clung to Chuck, brushing his hair, gently touching his face, staring stupidly at the blood on his shirt.

"He's dead." Her words were devoid of emotion.

"He should've stayed put," Carney said.

Frank Makins returned, ahead of a swish of wind and rain. "That piece of junk won't start."

Carney looked at the woman. "We tried to tell you. . . . You wouldn't let us talk. . . ."

"Let's stay here," Makins suggested.

"They're not far behind," Carney said.

"How do you know?"

Carney's patience had worn thin. "I know! You know! Every damn body knows!"

"It's only a kid and a nigger," Makins said. "We can wait here and surprise them."

Carney laughed dryly. "Two weeks ago you almost pissed your pants because you thought that kid was Cain, now

185

you find out he's black and you ain't scared anymore. You wait if you want. I'd rather tackle these Texas crackers." Without another word he turned and went out the front door. Makins hesitated a moment, then followed.

Pogo came out of the kitchen. He had heard it all. He sucked his fingers and looked around the room. The man was still on the floor, but there was no sign of the woman. Light came from the bedroom and he grinned. Those other fools could run around in the rain if they wanted to. He'd stay here and comfort the pretty young widow.

When her figure filled the bedroom doorway, Pogo's grin faded. She held a shotgun tightly against her shoulder, the knuckles on her hand white where she gripped the barrels. Pogo had time for one thought before she pulled both triggers—she wasn't so pretty after all.

(14)

The storm didn't let up until the next morning. By the time Roger and Cain reached the farmhouse it was full daylight. The sun was still low and the silhouette of the house shaded the back yard. A door was open, but no one was in sight. Roger held the rifle waist high.

"What do you think?"

"Only one way to find out." Cain started across the yard.

A dark haired woman with a shotgun stepped through the doorway. There was blood on her face and arms and her hair splayed out in wild disarray. Cain stopped while she inspected him.

"What do you want?"

Cain relaxed. At least she was thinking coherently. He didn't believe she would shoot, but if she did, it would be out of fear not deliberation. "We're looking for three men."

A shadow moved across her face. "What do you want with them?"

They'd hurt her bad. She would need convincing. "We're going to kill them," Cain said simply.

She didn't even blink. "What about the man behind you?"

"His name is Roger Horton. He's with me."

"How can I be sure?"

"You can tell us to leave and we will," Cain said.

She looked at both of them for a long time. Finally, she lowered the shotgun and went back in the house.

They found Chuck and Pogo in the living room. The woman sat on the sofa, looking at nothing, with Chuck's shotgun across her lap. Her face was pale, but there were still no tears. Things had moved too fast for crying. Roger knelt over her husband.

"The bullet went clean through," Roger said, "and he was shot in the back."

Pogo was twisted sideways over the arm of an easy chair, one hand in a half upraised position, as if he had tried to stop the shotgun pellets from tearing his face apart. A blood spattered canvas bag hung on a shoestring around his neck. Cain pulled it away.

"We have to go, Miss," Roger said, but she acted as if she didn't even hear.

After they left she rose and went into the kitchen, still dragging the shotgun, not because she had any more use for it, only that she didn't want to set Chuck's shotgun down anywhere. She looked at the back door and smiled wanly. It was the first time it had been closed in hours.

(15)

After a mile Makins found himself way behind. He could hardly make out Carney's bulky frame. He broke into a trot, tripped over his own feet and fell on his face. A trenchant pain raced up his leg and he grimaced as he lifted his pants. When he saw a jagged piece of bone protruding through bluish flesh, a panic seized his heart.

"Carney . . ."

Carney came back. He carried the black valise in one hand, his .38 in the other. He smiled thinly. "Help me!" Makins pleaded. "I didn't know this would happen!"

Carney looked at him, but his silence quickened Makins' understanding. "You're not leaving me here for that nigger!" he screamed, and dug for his gun. Too late he realized he wouldn't get it out in time. "No! Wait. . . ." Carney used one bullet and he put it in Frank Makins' stomach. He walked away and didn't look back.

Carney moved through a wood of scattered alders. At the edge of the trees he stopped. He saw the Rio Grande, swollen from the previous night's rain, and men wearing khaki uniforms and carrying automatic weapons. He'd expected this, sure he could slip across after dark, but the two men behind him complicated things. They would be on him before night fall. The men at the river, the two coming from the north. . . . There wasn't much to think about. He

188

backtracked to a field of rocks and a steep, flat-topped hill.

The sun moved high, a shimmering yellow disc that scorched the earth. Carney waited behind a knee-high boulder. His clothes were soaked and perspiration from his forehead ran into his eyes and down the sides of his nose. Suddenly one man appeared in the rocks at the bottom of the hill. He carried a rifle and one of the sacks from the bank. Carney cursed and snaked backwards, scraping the black valise as he dragged it along the ground. He started to scramble up, but a raucous voice froze his intent.

"Drop it or die!"

Where was the choice? Charlie Madden's Angel of Death only delivered corpses. "Die now or fry later," Carney thought with an odd humor. He threw the valise over his shoulder and lunged after it. Before he was fully around two bullets ripped into his throat.

Roger heard the shots and wondered what they meant. After a moment of silence he started up the hill. At the top he stopped and looked around in puzzlement. Cain sat on a rock, caressing an evil looking Luger, while Carney Thompson writhed on the ground, gurgling blood from two holes in his windpipe. It was the first time he had seen Cain's gun.

"Why don't you finish him?"

"He'll die quick enough," Cain said quietly.

Carney gave a last violent twitch and lay still. "You're a damn animal!" Roger shouted. A wave of nausea swept over him and he bent double and vomited.

Cain laughed sickly and looked solemnly at the sky. "I am just His instrument and He wants everybody killed, sooner or later."

Roger looked up quickly and understanding flooded through him. He wiped his mouth. "Take the heroin," he said. "I'm not stopping you."

Cain nodded at the money and the rifle. "I'll need those too."

Roger stood up straight. He let the canvas sack fall, but not so Cain could have it. He held onto Fred Hartgrove's rifle. "I told you what would happen if you tried to take it from me again."

Cain laughed and pointed the Luger at Roger. "You'd rather die yourself than kill a man! Don't you know that by now?"

It was eerie, like being hypnotized by a cobra before he struck with his fangs. A man was getting ready to take his life and all he could do was watch it happen. But, instinct for survival functions even when the mind goes blank, and before Roger realized what he was doing he had tilted the rifle and fired from the hip.

Cain staggered to his feet, like a drunken man, then flopped down on his back. He rolled over, put a hand to his chest and stared stupidly at the blood seeping through his fingers. A fire in his breast roared hot, grew unbearable, while a singeing sun overhead almost blinded him. A Mephistophelian blackbird settled on a rock three feet away and watched him with apathetic eyes, as he shivered and jerked to death's truculent song. Then the feathered inspector was no sun at all. Roger sat down alongside of him and began to cry.

190